Praise for *The Quick-Start Guide to Finance*

"Culture, marketers, and many family traditions can lead us right down the road to a life of financial stress. As Dirk says, 'Common practice does not equal common sense.' Weddings, college, kids, cars, furniture, food, and houses can be the events of our greatest joy—or the tools of regret that keep us poor. Put yourself in the driver's seat with this practical book and live with freedom and joy!"

—Dan Miller
New York Times bestselling author, *48 Days to the Work You Love*

"Dirk is an ordinary average guy who has taught himself how to win with money. If you're tired of debt or want to learn how to stop living paycheck to paycheck and build wealth, you must read this book. Dirk is completely transparent because he shows his previous debt and first actual budget. His information is not only easily categorized for reference but also his personal stories keep it relatable. Read this book at the risk of becoming successful with money."

—Roger White
Award-Winning Speaker, Author, and Entrepreneur

"Living high on the hog making your minimum credit card payments every month? Read this book. It will change the way you think. Dirk has personally conquered high credit card debt and here he outlines exactly how you can too!"

—Wendy Uken, Enrolled Agent
Tax Resolution Expert and Host of *Tax Tribe the PodCast*

"*The Quick-Start Guide to Financial Success* is loaded with wisdom and understanding from a guy who is getting it done and helping others to do so as well. Dirk's lessons learned can help readers avoid traps and pitfalls some of us have learned about the hard way! It is one of those books that you will be able to pull off the shelf over and over again to help make smart, practical financial decisions at key moments for the rest of your life. A great tool for financial success!"

—Patrick Green
MBA and author of *The Millionaire Journey*

"Dirk has written a heartfelt, wise, honest, and much-needed book. It can be enormously helpful both to those facing overwhelming debt and for those who would like to live their lives debt free and is a poignant, easy-to-follow road map to ensure a wonderful life for readers of *every age*!"

—Larry Mauthe
Husband, Father, and Executive Chef

DIRK MAIERHAFER

THE
QUICK-START
GUIDE TO

FINANCIAL
$UCCESS

Stop Struggling and Start Winning with Money!

The Quick-Start Guide to Financial Success
© 2019 Dirk Maierhafer

Published by Privateering Press, an imprint of Insignis Interactive, Inc.

ISBN-13: 978-1-946730-09-1 (hardcover)
ISBN-13: 978-1-946730-08-4 (paperback)

Edited by Jennifer Harshman, HarshmanServices.com
Cover and Book Design by James Woosley, FreeAgentPress.com

Published by Privateering Press
PrivateeringPress.com
Satsuma, Alabama 36572
VID: 20200802

AUTHOR'S NOTE

Life can be challenging. Especially when it comes to your financial life, *you can struggle* and try to figure it out on your own, *or* you can use a guide to get through them quickly.

The choice is yours.

This guide can help you make better financial decisions and help you create a path to *your own* financial success.

The information is easy to understand and easy to reference, allowing you to take quicker action throughout the different stages of your financial life.

This guide follows life's typical progression of financial milestones that kids, adults, and parents will likely face at some point in your life.

TABLE OF CONTENTS

About the Author ix

Acknowledgments xi

Introduction xiii

Chapter 1: Why Change? The Normal Is Fine. 1

Chapter 2: What's Your Definition of Financial Success? 3

Chapter 3: History Will Repeat Itself, Repeat Itself, Repeat Itself. Will You? 7

Chapter 4: Lack of Financial Education is By Design 9

Chapter 5: The Journey to a Fatter Wallet 13

Chapter 6: A Winning Mindset 29

Chapter 7: What's Your Money Situation? 35

Chapter 8: Hey! Where Did All My Money Go? (Your Paycheck and Withholdings) 47

Chapter 9: Your Financial Scorecard (Credit Reports, Credit Scores, and Identity Theft) 51

Chapter 10: Planning to Win (Budgeting & Financial Strategy) 55

Chapter 11: Quick and Easy Financial Wins 71

Chapter 12: I'll Pay for That Later! (Credit Cards) 73

Chapter 13: I Can't Drive 55! (Car Insurance and Buying That New Ride) 81

Chapter 14: A Temporary Situation (Moving, Renters Insurance, and Renting Basics) 93

Chapter 15: College Knowledge 101

Chapter 16: Walking Down the Aisle 109

Chapter 17: To Will or Not to Will, That is the Question 111

Chapter 18: Kids Are Really Expensive! 115

Chapter 19: My Home is My Castle (Insuring, Funding, and Picking the Right Home for You) 117

Chapter 20: Taking Care of Business (Other Types of Insurance
        You Need or Need to Know About) 133

Chapter 21: Start with The End in Mind! (Planning for Retirement and Investing) 145

Chapter 22: The Crossover (Funerals and Burials) 171

Chapter 23: Now What? Your Definition of Financial Success Revisited 175

Chapter 24: What's Your Plan? 179

Conclusion: The Next Challenge 183

ABOUT THE AUTHOR

Dirk Maierhafer

DIRK MAIERHAFER HAS ALWAYS been a dollars-and-cents guy, looking for deals and ways to stretch a dollar just a little more. Not only has he done this for his own personal finances, he has also done this for his clients. As of April 2019, he has managed a little over 709 million dollars for his clients, many of whom constantly rank in the top 40 of Fortune 500 companies. He is continuously looking for more efficient and effective ways to save and stretch available funding. It is not always easy or popular, but when you only have a specific amount of dollars to work with—well, that is all you have to work with. On one specific occasion, he proposed a solution that would save tens of thousands of dollars and the government agency that was involved stated that no one has ever proposed such a creative solution to this issue before. At one point during his travels, he decided to jot down a few ideas on finances that would have been very helpful at different financial stages in his life.

Eventually, he thought, *What if I created a quick-reference guide to help make financial decisions that was easy to understand, easy to implement, and could be used at any point in a person's life? How many people could benefit from a guide like that? How many lives could be changed for the better? What kind of opportunities could this create? And most of all, how many dreams could be fulfilled?*

Out of those questions came that which you now hold in your hands: *The Quick-Start Guide to Financial Success.*

Mission Statement

My personal mission is to help you make better financial decisions throughout your life. Through easy-to-understand information and real-life examples, you will be able to reach your dreams faster than you ever thought possible, while having a better life than you could have imagined.

ACKNOWLEDGMENTS

I **WANT TO THANK MY** wife Madalyn for all of the support and encouragement she has given me throughout the process of writing this book. I know it wasn't easy on you, Madalyn, but it's helped me to keep moving forward and complete a *huge* goal. I couldn't have done this without you, so thank you.

I would be remiss if I didn't thank my mom, Darlene, for all of the obvious reasons. Mom, I specifically want to thank you for inspiring me to help others understand the benefits of a budget while easing your worries of where you stand financially in retirement.

Larry, you have been an important part of my life ever since we met. I can't thank you enough for allowing me to be part of your family. I will never forget the adventures we had at Jellystone. Golf cart races, weed whackers, and "Normal" road trips. Ah, good times!

A special thank you to the talented Jennifer Harshman and her editing team for doing such an awesome job making sure I had—or more specifically, my first book had—the proper punctuation in all the right places.

And of course, a special thank you to the artistry of James Woosley for creating an eye-catching cover design and making the outside match the inside.

Finally, a special shout out to our dog, Mocha, who was always ready to play and forced me to take a break from writing when I needed it most. RIP 1/1/2019.

INTRODUCTION

THE QUICK-START GUIDE TO *Financial Success* will help you with life's financial challenges, such as getting out of debt, buying a car, paying for college, buying a house, saving for retirement, and many other financial milestones that will have a lifelong impact on you and your family. Unfortunately, there is a lack of basic financial education being taught in today's world, and this is one of the biggest reasons people are struggling financially. But you can have a better life. I wanted to write a book that could be handed out to anyone at any point in their life that would be easy to understand and useful for anyone to get started in making sound financial decisions. *The Quick-Start Guide to Financial Success* book starts to fill in the gaps to make your life easier along the way.

Nowadays, not many things come with a manual, just a quick-start guide. But I have never seen a quick-start guide for financial success. Have you? Isn't that kind of strange? Each of us uses money every day in some form, but you need to ask yourself how did I learn to use money? Do you know how to use money to your advantage and make great financial decisions? It may be something overlooked because money is so common that it is often assumed that everyone knows how to properly use money. I believe this book can help get you started on the path to making better financial decisions throughout your life. I also hope you start looking at which changes you can make today so you're able to have a better financial future.

I truly believe you can be financially successful if you have a guide, a path to follow, and a starting point. You will first need to establish what your definition or vision of financial success is at this point in your life. You will then need the correct mindset. Finally, you will need to believe in yourself and that you will be able to reach your definition or vision of financial success.

The Quick-Start Guide to Financial Success is a book of concentrated information without the fluff or fillers like other books. It gets you out of the starting blocks quickly, so you're able to see progress right away. Look, we have all made mistakes with money. These mistakes cost both time and, well, money, and in some cases years and years of headaches or arguments. Imagine if you could make better financial decisions the first time around, rather than make mistakes and then having to learn from them. How much further ahead would you be, could you be, if you could do it right the first time?

Look, I know how you feel and the stress you're under. I have been where you are, living paycheck to paycheck, making mistakes with money (and not knowing they were mistakes), taking out loans, buying things on credit yet thinking I was doing great! That was until I lost my job and boy, did things change and quick. Our two-income family went down to one. I was definitely stressed about money. Fortunately, my wife had a job and we were able to stay afloat, although it put a strain on our marriage during that time. Funny thing is, after I got a job again, we did not make many changes, but we did keep a closer eye on what we spent. We still had two car payments and a first and second mortgage on our house along with credit card bills. It still did not really sink in that when you have debt, you are at risk of losing everything (even if you do not really own it).

I always heard the "financial experts" on TV saying how you need 3 to 6 months of expenses saved for a rainy day. I thought to myself, *Well, that is easy for you to say. You don't have my bills and you have a job.* The thing is, I don't recall the financial experts giving examples or resources on the first steps you need to take to be able to save the 3 to 6 months of expenses they were talking about. A few more years went by before we got sick and tired of arguing about money and decided to change how we handled our money.

Fast forward to the present. I now can tell you where all our income has gone for the last 11 years. Some of you may be thinking, *Wow, that's impressive*, while others of you may be thinking *So what?*, and some of you may be trying to remember how much you spent today. Today we have no debt *at all* and, 9 months of expenses saved. Guess what—we don't need as much money now as we did as when we were in debt. Kind of weird how that works. We have always made investing for our retirement a top priority, but now that we are able to max out saving for retirement, we are also able to invest outside of our retirement accounts.

My wife was able to quit a high-stress job that was unfulfilling and take a year off to decompress and search for a new job that makes her happy and is fulfilling. If we had not made the changes in how we handled our money, we would have been in the same boat we were before. You can have so many more options and opportunities when you have financial freedom, and you do not have to worry about making it to the next paycheck.

I know you can do it, too. You just need a little guidance on how to get started. Life is so much better now than when we were in debt! Who doesn't want a better life with the financial freedom to be able to do what you want in life without the burden of financial obligations stopping you from living life and reaching your dreams? I can promise you that with the right mindset, goals, and actions, you will achieve financial success. Ask yourself what it would look like if you had financial freedom and financial success. What could you do? What would you do?

You are worth the effort! Your family is worth the effort! So, let's get you started and on your way to financial success! What are you waiting for? You can start today and change your future!

NUTSHELL

I have been in your shoes. Living paycheck to paycheck is stressful. I bought into the illusion that I was doing great with money because I could pay my bills and had a little cash left over each month. Unknowingly making poor financial decisions will continue if you are unwilling to face the truth of your financial reality. Change can be hard, but it is much easier if you tie the change to a cause or a reason that will keep you motivated and on track. My wife and I have changed our mindset on how to use money and set financial goals. We also took action that we have followed through to completion. Knowing where you are spending your money is as important as how much you are spending. Having money set aside for emergencies will reduce your financial stress, and being able to invest outside of your retirement accounts is how you can reach your financial success.

CHAPTER 1

Why Change?
The Normal Is Fine.

CHANGING THE WAY YOU normally go about making financial decisions can be difficult, but making small changes will make a huge difference throughout your journey.

Starting with the end in mind and working backward to figure out how you're going to start is the key. In other words, a goal, a target, or an objective is your end. Now you have to figure out how to get to where you want to be.

> When I was younger, I heard the phrase, "Start with the end in mind," but never understood it until later in life. I guess that is something we all need to think about when we're trying to teach someone something new. Ask them if they understand and have them explain it back to you so you can confirm that you are on the same page. And for those who don't understand something, raise your hand and ask questions until you do understand it. That is your responsibility and no one else's.

The Why

Why is financial success helpful in your journey through life? Are your financial obligations stopping you from living your life to its fullest and putting your dreams just out of reach? Are your dreams important? Yes, they are! Dreams can drive you to be better. Dreams can point you in the direction you should be going. Dreams can also cause an emptiness or a feeling like something is missing. So, how important are your dreams to you? Are they just about you, or are they bigger than you? Reaching your idea of financial success makes reaching your dreams much closer and accessible. How would that change your life, your family's life, your community, or the world? Your dreams are worth having, are they not? Stop asking why and start asking why not.

The How

I'm sure you're asking, "How can this book help me and/or how can I achieve financial success?"

Making sound financial decisions is how you achieve financial success. Begin with the basics, starting with the end in mind. Ask yourself, "Where do I want to be or end up?" Having the correct mindset is an absolute must before you can move forward. Setting targets or goals is next. You will finish up with a little adding and subtracting so you can achieve your target or goal.

In addition, working with the facts and removing the emotional impulses when you make financial decisions will help you reach financial success faster than any other single item. Just think back to when you made a medium or large emotional purchase. Did it end well, or are you wishing you would have made a different choice? When we make purchases and emotions are involved, we tend to justify poor decisions—and in most cases, these are in fact not sound financial decisions. They are emotional financial decisions.

Mindset, goals, and actions are how you will achieve financial success.

The What

Perhaps you are asking yourself, "What can *The Quick-Start Guide to Financial Success* book really do for me?" Well, you will gain a basic understanding of how you can make better financial decisions while building a solid foundation for the future. You will learn how to avoid the most common mistakes we make with money and often continue to make throughout our lives. You will learn how you can avoid getting into debt, stop incurring new debt, and most importantly, learn how to eliminate your existing debt. Remember, these are only the first steps to begin making better financial decisions and change the course of your life! That is a very big *what* in my eyes. What do you think?

CHAPTER 2

What's *Your* Definition of Financial Success?

MOST OF US HAVE our own definition or vision of what financial success looks like, but most often we are influenced by what others may have, what friends or family may say, or by what the talking heads on TV are telling us what financial success looks like.

Stop! This is about *you*! This is about *your* definition or vision of financial success and no one else's! This means you need to be crystal clear on what financial success looks like to you. This could mean a specific dollar amount in the bank, a specific lifestyle you want to have, or a specific place you want to live by a certain age.

Document your current definition or vision of financial success on the next two pages. Later, you can revisit them, as they will change over time, and might change after you finish this book.

Current Date: _____

_____

_____

_____

_____

_____

_____

_____

_____

_____

_____

_____

_____

CHAPTER 3

History Will Repeat Itself, Repeat Itself, Repeat Itself. Will You?

A FEW FAMOUS SAYINGS COME to mind regarding history.

*"Those who don't know history
are destined to repeat it."*

—Edmund Burke (1729–1797)

*"Those who cannot remember the past
are condemned to repeat it."*

—George Santayana (1863–1952)

We tend to have very short memories these days, especially when things are going well or appear to be going well. Let's take a quick look at the United States of America's financial history from its inception in 1776 to the end of 2018.

In the span of its 242 years, the United States has had approximately *47 recessions* or "downturns in the economy" that create hardships in the day-to-day lives of Americans who are not financially well off. A recession is defined by the *Merriam Webster Dictionary* as a period of temporary economic decline during which trade and industrial activity are reduced, generally identified by a fall in Gross Domestic Product (GDP) in two successive quarters. Recessions have lasted as little as 6 months and as long as 5 ½ years. Collectively, the recessions have spanned approximately *83 years*! Wow, 83 out of 242 years! That means since its inception, the United States has been in a recession approximately 34.29% of that time, or slightly more than ⅓ of its existence. Think about that for a little while. This should be one of those times you get that not-so-good feeling in the pit of your stomach. If not, you need to reread and really understand the math here.

Knowing this information, you can start to understand it's not a matter of *if* a recession will happen but a matter of *when* a recession will happen!

Living below your means, having an emergency fund of 6–9 months of expenses, being debt free, and reaching your financial success allows you to have financial freedom even during times when others are struggling. The Great Recession of 2008 has caused hardships that have lasted well beyond when experts and the government stated the recession was over.

What most people don't realize is that so much more has been lost financially as a result of people not being able to invest because they were unemployed or underemployed for years. This has caused a ripple effect far into the future. This means some of you will most likely need to work longer, causing you to retire much later than you could have if you had your financial house in order.

NUTSHELL

You will most likely experience at least one recession or "downturn in the economy" in your lifetime. Being prepared by living below your means, having an emergency fund of 6–9 months of expenses, being debt free, and reaching your financial success allows you to weather the storm no matter how long it lasts.

CHAPTER 4

Lack of Financial Education is By Design

MONEY IS THE ONE thing we use on a daily basis, but in most cases, we have little to no education on how to use it in a way that will truly benefit us during our lifetime. Doesn't that seem a little crazy? We're able to put plans together for vacations, parties, business trips, meetings, and all sorts of other things in our lives, but when it comes to putting a plan together for our own money, we have a huge blind spot. This is where the lack of financial education starts to show up.

Think back (for some of you it might be waaaaaaaaaay back), but has anyone ever sat you down and talked to you about money and how to use it? Did your mom, dad, grandma, or grandpa? My guess is probably not. You may have heard someone say, "Don't spend it all in one place," and that was the extent of your financial education. That's what I remember about my financial education.

This is a fundamental element in everyone's life, but it is not a focal point of any school that I'm aware of. Why is that? Really, why is that? Is this not an important subject that can make an impact on your entire life? Any thoughts to why that is?

Well, some of it is due to how the public-school system was designed. The public-school system was originally based off the Prussian education system, which was a factory-style system. It's an assembly-line type of education, treat everyone the same for each class, each grade, year after year. Take a look at how classrooms are set up—just like they were for factory workers back in the Industrial Revolution. That brings a little light to standardized testing, doesn't it? During that time, there was no expectation of higher education for us common folks, only for those who already had wealth. While there has been a shift for us common folks to continue our education, the public-school system has changed very little over the years. Why is that? The world has changed, but the way in which we are educated has not.

So, where and how did you learn about using money? As with most topics, you took in the information available to you from your immediate surroundings, and you learned it from watching your family and friends as well as others around you. If your family and friends go about their lives using money blindly and without a plan, the odds are you will start doing the same thing with your money as they do, because that's your normal. If your family has struggled with money for as long as you can remember, you are probably going to follow the same path. From time to time, the opposite happens, and someone does a 180-degree about-face. The person decides they will never live the same way they did as a kid, but that doesn't happen often. Most of the time, we never ask how we can improve our own education about money in a way that will benefit us during our lifetime. That's because the people around us are most likely in the same situation as we are, so there's no new or better information available, just the same old, same old.

We tend to talk in general terms about money. Discussing the specifics about what you should do with your paycheck seems to be taboo. But how are we going to learn if we don't talk about it or ask for help from someone that has a proven track record who is outside of your circle of influence? It seems like we are just supposed to know this without any guidance, but that's not how it works. Nothing works like that.

Just curious: what are you doing with your paycheck? Are you saving more of it than you're spending? My bet is that you're spending more than you're saving—if you're saving at all. Right? That's the normal around you. Just because you see someone with a big house and new cars doesn't mean they own any of it. They are most likely making bigger payments. That's all. They make more money, but in most cases, they make bigger financial mistakes.

NUTSHELL

If you are saving, that's awesome. Keep it up, and bump it up! If not, it's time to start. Be intentional with your money. Know where it's going. Discussing your financial specifics helps everyone to be on the same page in the same book with regard to your finances.

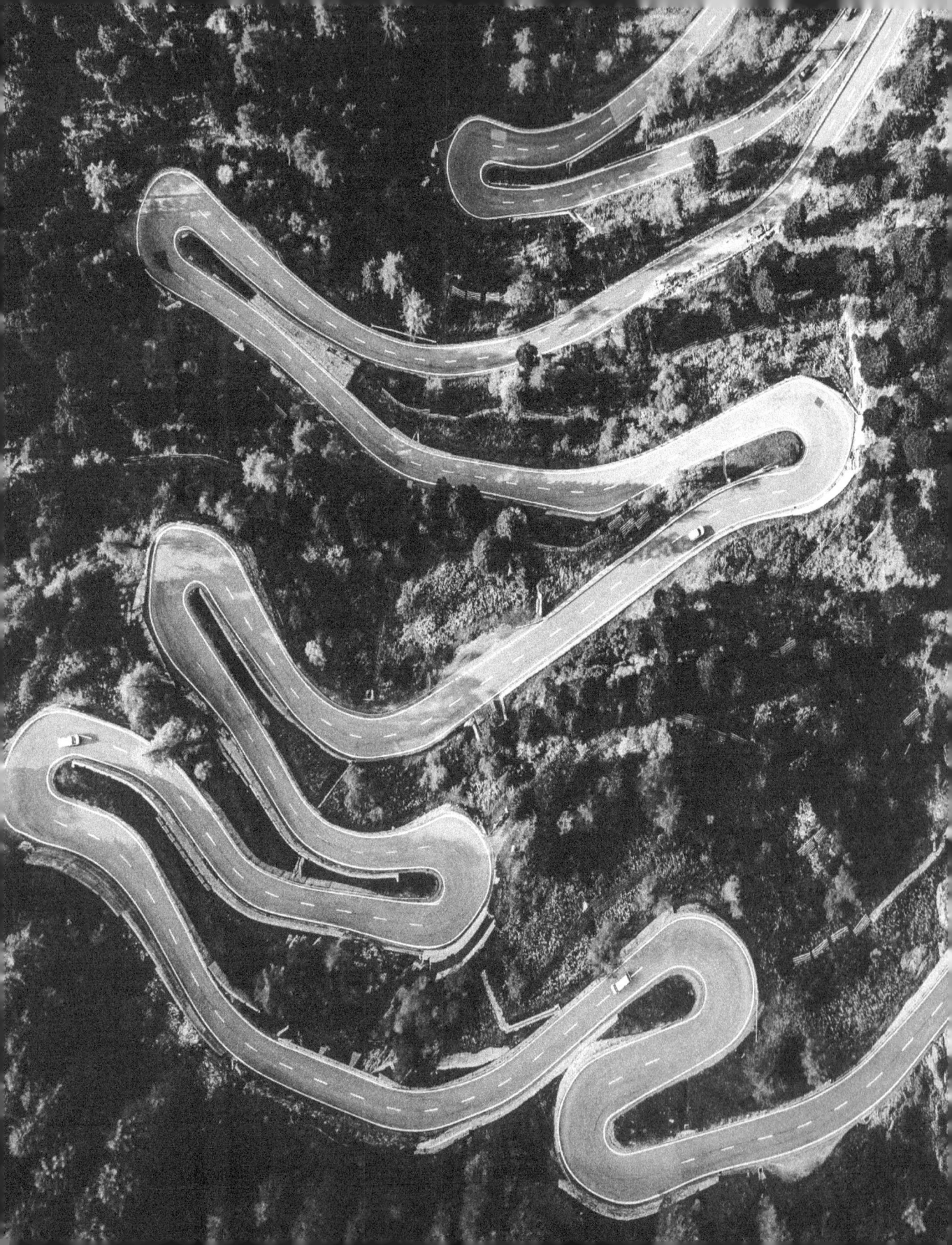

CHAPTER 5

The Journey to a Fatter Wallet

I'LL GIVE YOU A snapshot of my most recent financial history. Then I'll roll the calendar back and give you more insight into my journey to a fatter wallet.

I've been in project management for over 15 years. I've managed thousands of projects and a little over 709 million dollars for big-box retailers, restaurant chains, and discount stores. Do you know what they all have in common? Each project had a budget. I have yet to hear a client say, "We have a project we need you to manage, but don't worry about the cost. Money is no object, so there's no need to worry about staying within budget." I can tell you that's never going to happen, because it's always about the money! Regardless of who the client is, the one thing all projects have in common is a budget.

So why is it that you don't think you need a budget? Businesses use budgets to control and track costs and to make sure they are going to be profitable. Makes sense, right? Wouldn't it make sense for *you* to also have a budget in order to control your costs and make sure you're profitable? Most of us try to leave work at work, but in some cases, we need to take what we have learned at work and apply it to our own lives to be successful.

Okay, let's roll back the calendar to the early 1980s. Wow, I don't feel old, but writing that out sure makes me sound like I'm old . . .

I grew up in Fremont, Wisconsin, a small town with a population of just over 500 people. The kind of town where everybody knew everybody, and everybody knew everybody's business. It's a small-town thing—you wouldn't understand if you grew up in the big city. We lived in the country about 3–4 miles from town, but my parents owned a small grocery store in town, and of course I had to help out (not that I wanted to or got paid to). I stocked shelves, swept floors, brought grocery carts in from the parking lot, and so on. For all the years I helped out, the one thing we never talked about was money or how important a budget is to make sure you know what money was coming in and what money was going out for expenses. And we didn't talk about making sure the business was profitable. I could understand not talking about the budget for the business, but why would we not talk about our family budget? That would have been a handy bit of information. I wish I would have known what a budget was back then. I'm sure I would have been a lot better off later in life if I had. Maybe my parents didn't think it was important for me to learn at that time or maybe they weren't doing a budget at that time either.

> The reason I bring this up is learning how to use a budget, how to handle money, and how to stay out of debt is an important life skill that needs to be taught and learned at an early age. Unfortunately, this skill is lacking worldwide. It doesn't seem like people have learned anything from the job losses or economy shrinking after the terrorist attacks on 9/11/2001 or from the financial crisis of 2007–2008 that turned into The Great Recession that lasted from 2008–2012. It has taken many people and companies almost 10 years to get back to where they were 10 years earlier. This is also being referred to as the Lost Decade by some economists.

> A lost decade! Can you really afford to lose a decade of your financial life? A budget is a tool that can truly make a significant impact on how you live your life today and how you will be able to live your life in the future. What do you think? Does a budget seem like a good idea now?

Let's get back on track and rewind time back to the late 1980s (ages 15–16). Being a normal teenager of driving age, I obviously wanted to buy a car to further my independence rather than ride my bike into town to visit friends, go swimming, or go to work at the local campground. But I didn't have the money to buy my first car. By that time, my parents had divorced and a new (or new-to-me) car was not waiting for me when I turned 16, so that was a real bummer. But I really wasn't expecting one anyway, so it wasn't a huge let down. Nevertheless, I needed some wheels. I became really close with a family at the campground, and Larry was kind enough to loan me $1,000 to buy my very own car! We typed up a loan agreement, and I paid as agreed until the debt was paid off.

> Not knowing about a budget started me down a road I was not prepared for. Not having the money to buy a car to begin with should have been my first clue, and it was one that I obviously ignored. I should have waited until I saved the money to buy a car or at least a car I could have paid for in cash.

Fast forward to the early to mid 1990s (ages 19–23).

I was working full-time and investing in my 401k (I didn't really understand how the 401k worked, but I was always told to invest when you're young, so I did). I was going to college part-time, paying for it as I went along to keep from having a bill that would come due at a later date; I was also making a car payment and paying rent. At the time, I had $500 in savings, and all was right with the world. After getting a new job and making good money, I did what anyone would do. I went out and bought a new car with a loan. It was a shiny black 1994 Pontiac Grand Prix with all the bells and whistles. It was an awesome, fun, and fast car to drive! I could see myself driving it for years to come.

Little did I know fate had other plans. Later in the summer of 1994, I was in a car accident and was off work for months. Fortunately, the accident was not my fault, so everything was covered by the other driver's insurance. In the end, I received a small settlement out of it. After my recovery, I went back to work. After getting back on my feet, I thought, *Hmm, what should I do with the settlement money*? I ended up making a poor decision financially: I went out and bought a new truck to replace my car. I justified my new purchase by claiming I would be safer in a truck as they sit up much higher than a car. Again, I did not have all the funds to pay for my new truck, so I took out another loan to cover the difference.

> Hindsight is always 20/20. I never should have taken out a loan to buy a new car in the first place. I should have saved up and bought a used car with cash instead. And then I made another poor financial decision by purchasing a new truck with my settlement money. The smart play would have been to take a small portion of the settlement to buy a used truck and invest the rest.

Moving on to the mid to late 1990s (ages 24–27).

In December of 1994, I went on my first vacation, a cruise to the Caribbean, where I met my beautiful soon-to-be wife, who was from upstate New York. We talked for hours and hours throughout our vacation, and at the end of the cruise, we exchanged numbers and promised to keep in touch. Well, we did keep in touch and dated long distance for 2½ years. During that time, we paid for long-distance phone bills (this was before reasonably priced cell phones and cell phone plans), plane tickets, rental cars, and hotel rooms.

Besides traveling back and forth to spend time together, we also took trips and vacations together each year. As our relationship continued to grow, I could see an engagement ring would be next. She moved to Wisconsin in 1996, following our engagement. We rented a two-bedroom apartment that we "needed" to furnish; we used our credit cards to buy what we wanted. After settling in our new apartment, we decided we needed newer vehicles. I proceeded to take out a loan for a new truck, and she took out a loan for a newer car.

Dirk says . . .

EACH OF US HAS 24 HOURS PER DAY—168 HOURS PER WEEK—8,760 HOURS PER YEAR. HOW WILL YOU SPEND YOUR TIME?

> We justified renting a two-bedroom apartment just in case friends or family came to visit. They would need a place to sleep, right? The thing is we live close enough that our friends and family never stay over, but we still had to pay for the two-bedroom apartment. A smarter move would have been renting a one-bedroom apartment instead.
>
> Buying another new truck and a newer car and taking out loans on both of them was a pair of poor financial decisions that should have been avoided. Saving up to buy newer vehicles with cash would have been a much smarter financial decision.

As long as we thought we were doing so well, we decided to buy our first house—well, not really buy, as that would imply that we had the cash to actually *buy* the house. We did what anyone who didn't have the money to buy a house would do: we took out a mortgage. You know, "the normal way to buy a house."

We had very little for a down payment, so we had to pay PMI (private mortgage insurance) over and above our monthly mortgage amount. We continued to go out to eat and go on vacation using our credit cards, thinking life was good and we were on track to living the American Dream.

Several years later, I lost my job. That caused friction in our marriage due to the financial burdens of having two car payments, a mortgage payment, and several credit card payments. Fortunately, my wife had a job, and we were able to make it through until I got another job.

> Having at least 20% of the cost of the purchase price of the house would have saved us from having to pay private mortgage insurances (PMI). This is a non-payment/loan default protection for the *lender*, not for you. However, you have the privilege of paying for this insurance until your mortgage is at or below 20% of the home's value.
>
> Warning! PMI will not automatically be removed when you hit that magical 20% equity. You actually have to ask to have it removed! You might be paying for it right now and not even need it. We also should have saved to go on vacation instead of using a credit card. By making the above changes, we would have had more disposable income to pay off our loans and credit cards, and we could have started investing more at an earlier age.

Moving on to the early to mid 2000s (ages 28–33).

Shortly after the terrorist attacks of September 11, 2001, I again lost my job. As before, this created friction in our marriage due to the financial burdens of having two car payments, a mortgage payment, and several credit card payments. Again, fortunately, my wife had a job and we were able to make it through until I got another job. That time was different because the job was located in Forest Park, Georgia, just south of Atlanta. We made the choice to move from Wisconsin down to Georgia. The company my wife worked for had an office in Atlanta, and she was able to transfer.

We sold our house for a small profit and moved to Georgia. Instead of buying a house right away, we moved into an apartment for about 1½ years. This gave us time to figure out where we really wanted to live in the Atlanta area before we bought a house. This was a very smart move on our part, as we didn't know the area or the traffic patterns.

We eventually found an area we liked and purchased a house. But, based on the advice of the mortgage broker, we used very little of the proceeds we gained from the sale of our previous house. (A mortgage broker is not the best person to get advice from when they are loaning you money! The more money you are asking for, the more money the bank will make off you on commissions and interest). We did an 80/15/5 mortgage, which means our 1st mortgage was 80% of the home's value, and the 2nd mortgage was 15% of the home's value, leaving only 5% of the home's value that we needed to put down. This did help us avoid PMI (private mortgage insurance), and that was a good thing.

> This was a time when banks were lending money to anyone and everyone with a pulse. This later paved the way to the financial crisis of 2007–2008, which turned into The Great Recession from 2008–2012.

As before, we needed to furnish our new home, so we used credit cards to buy what we wanted. We had paid off our cars by then, but we decided to buy a newer used car for my wife to upgrade to (or "fit in with") our new surroundings and keep up with our peers. Again, we continued to go out to eat and go on vacation using our credit cards, thinking life was good.

Can you see the pattern and the repeated money mistakes that we made over and over again? I couldn't see it at the time, but looking back, it's so easy to see how we were making our financial decisions by thinking that was the normal thing to do to get what we wanted, when we wanted. How easy it would have been to change our habits had we been doing a budget and tracking where our money was going!

> We should have stayed in the apartment for a little longer, allowing us to save up a much larger down payment for our next house. We should have shifted our focus to paying off our car loans and our credit cards before even thinking about buying our next house. These changes would have given us more disposable income.

Moving on to the late 2000s (ages 34–37) . . .

At the time, we were not really paying attention to the news or reports about a financial crisis starting to unfold, due to the subprime mortgage lending practices in the banking industry. The signs were there years earlier, but most of us couldn't see the forest for the trees. By the time the red flags were raised in 2007, it was the beginning of the end that would turn into The Great Recession. Around the same time, we were starting to focus on our finances. We finally got fed up with fighting about money, making numerous payments, and living paycheck to paycheck. We finally got on the same page and formed a plan. We created a budget in March of 2008, so we could break the cycle of living paycheck to paycheck.

The hardest part was taking an honest look at the amount of debt we had accumulated and what we had done to get there. This was not a blame game—we both contributed to our debt issue. We needed to take responsibility for where we were financially. It would have been really easy to blame each other, but what good would that have done? We did have a few heated debates about our debt, but we realized that would not fix our problem and it was *our* problem. We needed to be held accountable for our financial actions moving forward.

First, we had to figure out how much money we were taking home each month. That worked out to be $5,425.60 a month. That was just take-home pay, not our total salaries, which were reduced by Federal, state, Social Security, and Medicare taxes, medical, dental, and vision insurance, long- and short-term disability insurance, and retirement contributions. Depending on our tax withholdings, the costs and types of insurances we chose, as well as the percentage we chose to contribute to each of our retirement plans, we could raise or lower our take-home pay at almost any time.

The second thing we needed to figure out was how much debt we had.

	Amount Owed	Interest Rate	Minimum Payment	Actual Payment
Car Loan 1	$ 7,720.69	4.9%	$ 475.00	$ 950.00
Car Loan 2	$ 11,894.97	5.9%	$ 400.00	$ 400.00
1st Mortgage	$ 102,850.55	5.9%	$ 650.69	$ 650.69
2nd Mortgage	$ 6,429.55	5.4%	Interest Only	$ 100.00
Credit Card 1	$ 2,783.31	12.0%	$ 65.00	$ 2,783.31
Credit Card 2	$ 1,525.08	15.0%	$ 40.00	$ 1,525.08

Total in Car Loans	$ 19,615.66	**TOTAL DEBT:**	
Total in Mortgages	$ 109,280.10	**$133,204.15**	
Total in Credit Cards	$ 4,308.39		

After adding it all up, we found that we were **$133,204.15** in debt! This was obviously a far cry from being on track to living the American Dream . . .

Our take-home pay was $5,425.60 a month, and we were spending $2,100.69 a month on two mortgages and two car loans. That's 38.7% of our income gone, right off the top! That left us with $3,324.91 or 61.3% of our remaining take-home pay. Well, that doesn't sound so bad, right? But we still needed to pay for everything else out of that $3,324.91: food, clothes, utilities, and personal care items. Not to mention we still needed to pay for gas, car maintenance and/or repairs, car insurance, homeowners insurance, home maintenance and/or repairs. Then we had out-of-pocket medical/dental bills, term life insurance, and credit card bills. All this was while building an emergency fund.

We found the biggest surprise was how much we were spending on going out to eat and how often we were going out to eat. You know what? Our waistlines were telling us the same thing, but we chose to ignore them as well. Our solution was to just buy larger clothes . . .

Dirk says . . .
COMMON PRACTICE DOES NOT EQUAL COMMON SENSE.

The next two pages will show you our first actual budget. If you're not familiar with a budget, this may be overwhelming or intimidating, but not to worry. I'll explain it in detail a little later on in the chapter "Planning to Win."

The numbers in parentheses ( ) show that we had gone over budget. As you can see, we did not have a balanced budget as clearly shown by the ($5,338.39) in the box next to Balanced Budget.

HOUSEHOLD INCOME	$5,425.60
TOTAL BUDGET	$10,763.99
BALANCED BUDGET	($5,338.39)

TOTAL SPENT SO FAR THIS MONTH	$10,858.21

WEEKLY TOTAL SPENT	$1,522.22	$1,016.13	$1,701.83	$6,618.03	$0.00
REMAINING CASH	$3,903.38	$2,887.25	$1,185.42	($5,432.61)	($5,432.61)

							$174.25	($94.22)
BUDGETED ITEMS	SPEND PLAN	$ SPENT Week 1	$ SPENT Week 2	$ SPENT Week 3	$ SPENT Week 4	$ SPENT Week 5	$ ACCUM	DIFFERENCE

EMERGENCY FUND RUNNING TOTAL			
3 Months	6 Months	9 Months	12 Months
-	-	-	-

COO = Cash Only Option

SAVING / INVESTING

BUDGETED ITEMS	SPEND PLAN	$ SPENT Week 1	$ SPENT Week 2	$ SPENT Week 3	$ SPENT Week 4	$ SPENT Week 5	$ ACCUM	DIFFERENCE
Emergency Fund	$1,000.00	$500.00	-	-	$500.00	-	$1,000.00	-
Savings	$0.00	-	-	-	-	-	-	-
Retirement Fund	$0.00	-	-	-	-	-	-	-
Investing	$0.00	-	-	-	-	-	-	-

HOUSING

BUDGETED ITEMS	SPEND PLAN	$ SPENT Week 1	$ SPENT Week 2	$ SPENT Week 3	$ SPENT Week 4	$ SPENT Week 5	$ ACCUM	DIFFERENCE
1st Mortgage	$650.69	-	-	-	$650.69	-	-	-
2nd Mortgage	$100.00	-	-	$100.00	-	-	-	-
Property Tax	$126.25	-	-	-	$126.25	-	$126.25	-
Homeowner's / Renters Ins.	$48.00	-	-	$48.00	-	-	$48.00	-
Furnishings	$0.00	-	-	$504.11	-	-	-	($504.11)

UTILITIES

BUDGETED ITEMS	SPEND PLAN	$ SPENT Week 1	$ SPENT Week 2	$ SPENT Week 3	$ SPENT Week 4	$ SPENT Week 5	$ ACCUM	DIFFERENCE
Electricity	$165.00	$163.05	-	-	-	-	-	$1.95
Water	$25.00	-	$21.81	-	-	-	-	$3.19
Cell Phone	$53.01	-	$46.94	-	-	-	-	$6.07
Home Phone / Internet	$61.05	-	-	$61.05	-	-	-	-
Trash	$31.00	-	$31.00	-	-	-	-	-
Paid TV Service	$64.99	-	$64.99	-	-	-	-	-

FOOD

BUDGETED ITEMS	SPEND PLAN	$ SPENT Week 1	$ SPENT Week 2	$ SPENT Week 3	$ SPENT Week 4	$ SPENT Week 5	$ ACCUM	DIFFERENCE
Grocery (COO)	$300.00	$152.01	$2.34	$107.05	-	-	-	$38.60
Restaurants Family (COO)	$120.00	$27.35	$21.40	$50.03	$15.56	-	-	$5.66
Restaurants Person 1 (COO)	$80.00	$80.00	-	-	-	-	-	-
Restaurants Person 2 (COO)	$80.00	-	-	-	-	-	-	$80.00
Other (COO)	$360.00	$100.00	$100.00	$40.00	$119.38	-	-	$0.62

AUTO								
Car Payment 1	$950.00	$100.00	$337.50	$237.50	$237.50	-	-	$37.50
Car Payment 2	$400.00	$100.00	$100.00	$100.00	$100.00	-	-	-
Vehicle Insurance	$205.43	-	-	$205.43	-	-	-	-
Gas / Oil (COO)	$458.00	$118.46	$220.15	$127.57	$51.44	-	-	($59.62)
Repairs / Tires / Maint. (COO)	$565.83	-	-	-	$283.00	-	-	$282.83
License / Taxes	$200.00	-	-	-	$182.78	-	-	$17.22
Vehicle Replacement	$0.00	-	-	-	-	-	-	-

CLOTHING								
Adults (COO)	$50.00	-	-	$42.33	-	-	-	$7.67

MEDICAL / HEALTH								
Health Ins / Doctor	$0.00	$30.00	$70.00	$30.00	$30.00	-	-	($160.00)
Prescription / Vitamins	$45.00	$60.00	-	-	-	-	-	($15.00)

PERSONAL								
Life Insurance	$91.35	$91.35	-	-	-	-	-	-
Hair Care (COO)	$15.00	-	-	-	-	-	-	$15.00
Gifts (Birthday / Christmas)	$30.00	-	-	-	-	-	-	$30.00
Fun Time (COO)	$60.00	-	-	-	$4.50	-	-	$55.50
Donations (COO)	$30.00	-	-	-	-	-	-	$30.00
Pet Care (COO)	$40.00	-	-	$42.24	-	-	-	($2.24)

FUN STUFF								
Entertainment (COO)	$50.00	-	-	$6.52	$8.54	-	-	$34.94
Vacation	$0.00	-	-	-	-	-	-	-

DEBT							Debt Owed
Master Card	$1,525.08	-	-	-	$1,525.08	-	$1,525.08
Visa	$2,783.31	-	-	-	$2,783.31	-	$2,783.31

> We realized we needed to change to our mindset and our habits in order to break the cycle of living paycheck to paycheck and have a brighter financial future. With our eyes newly opened, we could see we had been fooling ourselves into thinking life was good and we were on track to live the American Dream. The fact was, it was a lie we kept telling ourselves over and over until we believed it.

The late 2010s to the present (age 38+).

As we continued to follow our budget and live below our means, we started to see traction—our debt amounts were going down. This continued to give us hope and inspiration that *we could do this,* and we would be out of debt if we stuck to our new mindset, new habits, and our budget. I adopted the mantra of "short-term pain for long-term gain" when challenging and difficult choices needed to be made or when "I want . . . I deserve," popped up. If we hadn't made those tough choices, we would have been reverting back to trading our future for the present instead of trading our present for a better future.

> If you truly "deserve" something, you will have earned it, but remember no one said life was fair. You may "deserve it" and still not get it. The "I deserve" mentality can and will lead you to make very poor financial decisions. It can also lead to justification of your poor decisions. If you have truly earned it, great friends, family, and companies will recognize you for it.

One of the first things we made an adjustment to is the amount we set aside for going out to eat. We started at $280 per month. Previously, we went out to eat whenever we wanted and as many times as we wanted. Now we had to stay within the $280 we allotted for going out to eat. You may be wondering why I didn't include the $360 I used for work in the $280. When I traveled for work, I received a per diem allowance. However, I needed to pay for the meals out of pocket, and then I later received the per diem for the days that I had been traveling. It was easier to separate the money that I used for work rather than lump it in with nonwork eating out.

Within the first 2 months (April 2008), we paid off $4,308.39 in credit card debt and reduced our car loans by $1,900. Each month, we refined our budget, adjusting as needed to make the maximum dent in our debt. We kept in mind that irregular bills would be coming up such as home/auto insurance and real estate taxes. We even saved a little each month to pay those in full when they came due.

By the first week of the 5ᵗʰ month (July 2008), we had paid off car loan #1! The final payment was only $237.50. That left us $712.50 that we could apply toward other debts or save for upcoming bills. We immediately applied $475 to our 2ⁿᵈ mortgage, on which we had only been paying $100 monthly and getting very little traction, since we were paying just a bit more than the interest. With the increased payment, we would be paying a minimum of $575 each month, so we would be able to make headway on our 2ⁿᵈ mortgage moving forward.

Yes! Happy dance taking place! We suddenly had some breathing room! We could even start to save a little each month, so we could take a modest vacation by paying cash for it and not having to worry about a credit card payment when we got back.

For the first time, we started saving money for a vacation. Imagine taking a vacation but paying for it before you go! To this day, we continue to save for each of our vacations, meaning no credit card bills or headaches after our trips. We have been able to make every vacation a true no-worries vacation ever since.

By the 9ᵗʰ month (November 2008), we were able to make the final payment on our 2ⁿᵈ mortgage! Let's do a quick recap. We were going into our 10ᵗʰ month. We had saved $1,000 for our starter emergency fund, paid off all of our credit cards, car loan #1, and our 2ⁿᵈ mortgage. We also saved for our real estate taxes, our homeowners insurance, our car insurance, and some car maintenance/repairs. At month 10, we had freed up $1,050 per month that we used toward paying off our 2ⁿᵈ car loan.

By the 13ᵗʰ month (March 2009), we had made our last payment on car loan #2. We did use some of our savings to expedite paying off that loan. Once it was done, we shifted our focus to funding our emergency fund of 6 months of expenses.

By the 22ⁿᵈ month (December 2009), we had a 6-month emergency fund. In less than 2 years, we had paid off all our consumer debt except our house.

By the 23rd month (January 2010), we adjusted what we were paying on our first mortgage to $600 a month. We did that so we could save for our home/auto insurance and real estate taxes.

We continued to increase what we were paying on our mortgage whenever we could, starting on the 31st month (September 2010) to $700, then by increments over the next 5 years. We went from $900 to $1,050, to $1,150, to $1,200, and to $2,158. By the 95th month (February 2016), we had increased our monthly payment to a whopping $2,640 a month.

On the 98th month (May 2016), we paid off our house! We made the decision to use all but $100 of our emergency fund to pay off the house as well as all the money we had saved for our vacation home/auto insurance and real estate taxes. This was a little (a lot) scary, but we realized we would be able to rebuild a 6-month emergency fund and rebuild what we had saved for our vacation home/auto insurance and real estate taxes over the next 5 months.

By the 103rd month (October 2016), we had rebuilt our 6-month emergency fund as well as the funds we had previously saved for our vacation, home/auto insurance, and real estate taxes. Wow! What a journey! To be perfectly honest, it was a tough road at first, especially the first 3 months and even a few times along the way, but it was definitely worth it. Once we started using our budget as a tool and realized the power of knowing where, why, and what we were spending our money on, things started to fall into place financially. This has become *our* new normal. Through our journey, we found that "stuff" had less and less value and our financial freedom had the greatest value of all. The power to choose what we want to do with our future is now ours. In the end, we found that it's all just *stuff*!

When we were in debt, we didn't think much about taking out a loan to buy a big-ticket item or using our credit cards to take a vacation. We thought it was okay and that's what you did to get what you want. But as we paid off our debt, our mindset was also changing. As we got closer and closer to having *zero debt*, the temptations of the past were not even on our radar. We no longer got caught up in what our friends were doing or thought, least of all what they were buying. We had committed to each other that this was what we wanted. We supported each other and reminded each other why we were doing this when the tough decisions had to be made. Our future has more opportunities and more options available to us than ever before! The best part is that from this point on, every dollar we make is *ours* to save, invest, spend, or give *as we choose*! What about your future? Do you want more opportunities and more options in your life?

NUTSHELL

We started out **$133,204.15** in debt. **In 22 months (1.8 years), we had paid off $30,353.60** and were debt free except for our house. That averages out to $1,379.71 that we were paying toward our debt each month. We did use some savings to expedite paying off this debt, but it was money we had saved as we were getting out of debt.

Once we paid off our non-mortgage debt, that still left us with $102,850.55 of mortgage debt. However, I needed to adjust for the $3,041.15 that we paid off during the previous 22 months. So, $102,850.55 – $3,041.15 = $99,809.40.

In the next 75 months (6.25 years), we had paid off our remaining mortgage balance of $99,809.40. That averaged out to $1,330.79 that we were paying toward our remaining mortgage debt each month. We did use some of our savings to expedite paying off our mortgage, but it was money we saved while we were getting out of debt.

In 97 months (8.05 years), we were 100% debt free including our house.

In 103 months (8.75 years), we were 100% debt free including our house and had a 6-month emergency fund saved.

Just so you're not thinking we sat around the house and did nothing (although that's one way to spend less money and get out of debt), we took weekend trips and vacations during our journey to become debt free by simply adjusting our budget. Sure, sometimes we had to wait a month or two to get what we wanted, but that was okay with us because we knew what our financial goals were, and we knew that financial discipline was going to pay off in the end and for years to come. We actually have a line item in our budget for entertainment. That way, we were able to have money set aside to do fun things each month, even though it was a relatively small amount in the beginning. We rented movies instead of going to movies. We got takeout instead of eating in the restaurant, and we even started to exercise more and eat better. You need to be creative and resourceful and understand that what you're doing with your money is important and that you need a plan. Now that we're debt free, we're able to save, invest, and take several vacations a year. We have a great time at a great price. We shop around and stay at all-inclusive resorts or take a cruise—you're able to get more for less with these types of choices.

You may think you're just trading dollars for stuff when you spend your money, but what you're actually doing is trading your future for stuff!

THIS IS
THE SIGN
YOU'VE BEEN
LOOKING FOR

CHAPTER 6

A Winning Mindset

THE *OXFORD DICTIONARY* **DEFINES** mindset as, "The established set of attitudes held by someone."

In other words, your belief or approach about how you use money has formed over time, right or wrong. Well, I hate to be the bearer of bad news, but your mindset has been less than correct when it comes to money and how you can reach financial success. I'm sure you're thinking, *Well, yeah; that's why I bought the book*! Let's take a look at what you know about money and how you can reach financial success.

On the lines below, make a list of what you can do with money.

On the lines below, make a list of ways you can reach financial success.

Okay, now that you have made your list, let's look at what you can actually do with money. There are only four things you can do with money once you have it.

1. Save
2. Invest
3. Spend
4. Give

How many of the four are on your list? One, two, three, or all four? I'm guessing you had three of them. Did you look closely? These are listed in a specific order for a reason.

1. **Save.** You should always pay yourself first. But what does that mean, "Pay yourself first"? It means before anyone else is paid, you must set aside money for yourself. It may not be much at first, and that's okay, but you have to start somewhere, and it's better than nothing at all. Over time, this will grow to be a larger and larger amount.

2. **Invest.** To become financially successful, you need to invest. When you have money, you're able to do that. Take advantage of an employer's retirement plan or set up your own. We will get to the details on investing in the Start with The End in Mind chapter.

3. **Spend.** This is something we all can do just fine without any help.

4. **Give.** This can be to a charity, a church, or a friend.

Dirk Says . . .

WE ARE WHO WE CHOOSE TO BE BY THE CHOICES WE MAKE, SO CHOOSE WISELY.

Now we can look at how you are going to reach your financial success.

You probably listed a high-paying job, inheritance, saving, investing, or maybe winning the lottery as ways to reach financial success. Those are the *what* that can get you to financial success—but not the *how* to get you to financial success. A financial plan or a budget is the *how*.

How do you actually change your mindset?

1. Understand that you will need to modify your current way of thinking and most importantly understand why you want or need to change your mindset.

2. Making a conscious effort to change your mindset is key. It's just not going to happen without effort.

3. Start applying your new mindset.

4. Willpower and motivation will only take you so far. Have a plan in place, and keep repeating the steps.

5. Take small steps when you're starting out. Don't take too big of a step. That may cause you to fail and/or quit.

6. Don't give up when you stumble. Get back up, dust yourself off, and continue on.

Changing your mindset will not happen overnight. Be patient.

NUTSHELL

It will take real effort on your part to change your way of thinking on how to use money, but it also takes patience and time. Have a plan in place that you can follow even if life is going great, but especially when life gets tough! Life happens!

CHAPTER 7

What's Your
Money Situation?

THIS IS AN OVERVIEW of your financial status. This should help clarify any misconceptions that you may have had about where you truly stand financially, and in most cases, it will scare the %&*@ out of you! The truth hurts, and sometimes it's not very pretty! You now have your starting point. You can use this information to make the needed changes to become debt free, build wealth, reach your financial success, and have an awesome life.

For a more in depth look at your overall financial situation, pick up a copy of *The Quick-Start Guide to Financial Success Workbook* today.

WHY
Why don't you want to do a budget?

_____

_____

_____

_____

Why do you think a budget won't help you?

_____

_____

_____

_____

_____

_____

Why do you not have an emergency fund?

_____

_____

_____

_____

_____

_____

Why are you living paycheck to paycheck?

_____

_____

_____

_____

_____

_____

Why are you going to change your spending and savings habits?

_____

_____

_____

_____

_____

_____

HOW

How often are you going to create and review your budget?

How are you going to hold yourself accountable with the budget you have created?

How are you going to change your spending and savings habits?

How long will it be before you start your budget?

_____

_____

_____

_____

_____

_____

How are you going to stick to your budget when you're on vacation?

_____

_____

_____

_____

_____

WHAT

What is stopping you from starting a budget today?

_____

_____

_____

_____

_____

What are you going to change to stay on budget?

_____

_____

_____

_____

_____

Dirk says . . .

THE AVERAGE LIFE EXPECTANCY IS ABOUT 78 YEARS. THAT WORKS OUT TO 683,280 HOURS WITH A NORMAL 40-HOUR WORK WEEK. YOU WILL SPEND 35 YEARS OF THAT WORKING, OR 582,400 HOURS. DOES THIS PUT THINGS IN PERSPECTIVE?

STATUS

Are you living paycheck to paycheck?

Are you stressed out because you have more bills than money each month?

Are you and your significant other fighting about money?

What is your monthly take-home pay?

How much do you have in your savings?

Do you have $500–1,000 as a starter emergency fund?

Do you have back taxes you need to pay, if so, how much do you owe?

Do you have any credit card bills, and if so, how many credit card bills do you have?

- What is the current balance on each card, and what is the combined total amount?

- What are your monthly payments on each card, and what is the combined total amount?

- Do you pay them off every month? If not, what do you pay on them each month?

Do you have any car loans, and if so, how many loans do you have?

_____

_____

- What is the current balance on each car loan, and what is the combined total amount?

  _____

- What are your monthly payments on each, and what is the combined total amount?

  _____

Do you have any miscellaneous loans (boat, ATV, RV, motorcycle, etc.), and if so, how many?

_____

_____

- What are the current balances on each, and what is the combined total amount?

  _____

- What are your monthly payments on each, and what is the combined total amount?

  _____

Do you have student loans, and if so, how many do you have?

- Are they private, Federal, or both?

- What is the current balance on each student loan, and what is the combined total amount?

- What are your monthly payments on each student loan, and what is the combined total amount?

Do you have a mortgage?

- Which type of loan is it? Conventional, FHA, VA, USDA rural housing, adjustable rate mortgage (ARM), 203k, or home equity line of credit (HELOC)?

- What is the current balance?

- What is your monthly payment?

Do you have a second mortgage?

- Which type of loan is it? Conventional, FHA, VA, USDA rural housing, adjustable rate mortgage (ARM), 203k, or home equity line of credit (HELOC)?

- What is the current balance?

- What is your monthly payment?

Do you pay rent, and if so, what is your monthly payment?

Do you pay child support, and if so, what is your monthly payment?

Do you pay alimony or palimony, and if so, what is the monthly payment?

_____

_____

Do you have collection agencies calling you? List the names of the collection agencies:

_____

_____

_____

- What is the current balance of each amount owed?

_____

- What is your monthly payment on each amount owed?

_____

NUTSHELL

This is an in-depth view of your financial status. This should help clarify any misconceptions that you may have had about where you truly stand financially, and in most cases, it will scare the %&*@ out of you! The truth hurts, and sometimes it's not very pretty! You now have your starting point. You can use this information to make the needed changes to become debt free, build wealth, reach your financial success, and have an awesome life.

CHAPTER 8

Hey! Where Did All My Money Go?
(Your Paycheck and Withholdings)

GETTING PAID IS WHAT it's all about. That's why you do what you do to get that cold hard cash in your hot little hands! Right? Today's that day; it's payday! You're adding up all the money in your head and dreaming of what you're going to do with all of it. The boss hands you that freshly sealed envelope with that little window in front with your name showing through it, and in your head, you start to hear MONEY, MONEY, MONEY, MOOONNNAAAAAAAAAAAAAY, MONNAAY . . . But all of a sudden, the needle scratches across the record and makes the most awful sound like fingernails across a chalkboard. The music stops . . . Hey! Where the heck is the rest of my money?

This will probably be a shock to those who are getting their first paycheck. Once you've accepted a job, normally on your first day you filled out a lot of paperwork, whether it was on real paper or online. You probably filled out medical, dental, retirement investing, life insurance, short-term disability (STD), and long-term disability (LTD) forms, along with state and Federal withholding forms (at least in the United States). A form called a W-4 or an Employee's Withholding Allowance Certificate is a Federal (IRS) form required to be filled out by all employees. This allows the employer to withhold a specific amount of money (income tax) based on your allowances as stated on the W-4 form. Your employer sends this directly to the IRS. This is the tax you owe to the Federal government (IRS) on the gross income you earned. States have their own specific withholding forms that are also required to be filled out, but some states do not have state income tax, so no form or withholdings are required at the state level.

The forms are simple to fill out, but you want to ask your accountant or tax advisor each year if you need to adjust your withholdings for the new year. This may mean that you will get a smaller refund or you will pay a small amount of tax to the government, rather than just guessing and having to pay a large amount in at the end of the year. The more "allowances" that are listed on the W-4, the less money that will be withheld for taxes or the bigger the paycheck you will take home. This is great every time you get paid, but at the end of the year, after completing your annual income tax forms and realizing you have not paid in enough taxes, beads of sweat will start to form on your forehead as you try to figure out where you're going to get the extra money to pay those additional taxes. The IRS will come after you for back taxes. If you delay paying your taxes, the IRS will impose penalties and fees on top of the additional taxes that you owe. The IRS can and will seize your property as well as garnish your wages to obtain the taxes you owe.

On the other hand, if you have very few or no "allowances" or you have extra money withheld to ensure you have paid all of your tax obligations at the end of the year, you may find that the IRS owes you a refund. The bigger the better! Right? Wrong! While getting a refund sounds like a great thing, it's not. This money was yours to begin with. What you did was overpay the government, and they are just refunding the portion you overpaid. **You gave the government an interest-free loan for 12 months!**

Say you received a $6,000 tax refund last year. That's a nice little refund, right? But what if you're struggling each month and a few hundred dollars could change your life? An extra $500 a month would help you out quite a bit, wouldn't it? Having the incorrect amount of taxes withheld from each paycheck can cause you to struggle when you don't have to. What could you do with an extra $500 each month?

I don't know about you, but I would rather have that money in my bank account and not in the government's hands. We all know how well the government handles other people's money.

Paycheck Breakdown

Look at your paycheck a little closer, and start with gross income versus net income. Confused? Yeah, taxes, the government, and all the stuff in between can do that to you.

Gross Income

On a paycheck, it is simply all of the money that you have earned without anything being withheld or deducted.

For example, you work 80 hours at $35 an hour. That equals $2,800. **The $2,800 is your gross income**; nothing has been withheld or deducted from that amount.

Net Income

On a paycheck, it is simply the money left over after all the withholdings and deductions have been subtracted.

Your paycheck also should include a list of items that have been withheld or deducted. What remains is **your net income** or what is more commonly known as your take-home pay.

For example, you work 80 hours at $35 an hour. That equals $2,800. The $2,800 is your gross income. We now start subtracting your withholdings and deductions from that $2,800:

- Federal taxes $300
- State taxes $150
- Social Security $150
- Medicare $50
- Medical $250
- Dental $20
- LTD $10
- STD $10
- Retirement $450
- Vision $5
- Life insurance $25.

Your net income is $1,380.

$2,800 gross income (before withholdings and deductions)

–$1,420 withholdings and deductions

$1,380 net income (take-home pay or after withholdings and deductions)

If you're an independent contractor, sole proprietor, or non-employee, you will be responsible for your own withholdings and deductions, and you will receive a gross income check for the service that you provide.

Note

Always consult your accountant or tax advisor. Tax laws continually change and vary by state as well as by country.

NUTSHELL

Be aware of the withholdings and deductions that are taken out of your check. Adjust your withholdings each year to the point of being within a few dollars of your income tax bill. A refund is not the government giving you free money; it's *your money* that you overpaid to the government. You basically loaned the government your money for 12 months, and you don't get paid any interest.

CHAPTER 9

Your Financial Scorecard
(Credit Reports, Credit Scores, and Identity Theft)

YOU'RE PROBABLY ASKING THE following questions. What the heck is a credit report/ score? Why is this important? Where can I get one? How can it affect me? How is this information gathered and compiled?

A credit report is a statement about your current credit standing and credit activity. This is a way for banks, credit unions, credit card companies, mortgage companies, landlords, and even employers to evaluate how well you handle money. This helps these companies and institutions determine whether they want to take the risk to lend you money, and if so, how much money they're willing to lend you; whether they want to rent to you, or even to offer you a job. The report at its core tells other people and companies if you pay your bills, if you pay them on time, or how often you're late paying your bills.

One thing that you may not know is that your credit report may not be accurate, and the credit reporting agencies don't care. Equifax, Experian, TransUnion, and to a much lesser extent Innovis, package your information—right or wrong, good or bad—and sell it off to whoever wants to buy it. If your report has errors or incorrect information on it, it can dramatically impact your life. It could mean higher insurance rates, higher interest rates on loans, outright denials for credit, or denials of job offers. It is really scary that errors on your credit report could impact your life so much and that the companies selling your information are unable to guarantee that the information they are providing is 100% accurate.

How do you know if there are errors on your report? Well, you just need to pull your own credit report! This can be done for free at AnnualCreditReport.com. This is the only legitimate site where you're able to get a free copy of your credit report from each of the three major credit reporting agencies once each year. Here is more good news: you're able to dispute the errors that you may find on your credit report, although the process can be a little difficult.

Most banks and credit card companies are now providing you with your credit score on each statement. They pull it each month anyway, so it's marketed as a benefit to you. So, what is a credit score, and how do you get one? Your score is generated by using algorithms that look at:

- Payment history (35%)
- Amount of debt owed (30%)
- Length of credit history (15%)
- New credit (10%)
- Types of credit used (10%)

Credit scores range from as low as 300 to as high as 850.

Lenders view those with a higher credit score as less of a risk than those with a lower credit score. While a credit score doesn't give the whole picture about your financial past, this is how you are viewed, right or wrong, good or bad, and unfortunately in most cases, your credit score is viewed as an absolute.

Each time you apply for some type of credit, your credit score will go down for a short time. For example, you're just out of college and you've rented your first apartment. Other than your futon from college, you don't have any furnishings. You decide that you "need" all new stuff because you're an adult now, and that's what adults do. You apply for several credit cards, and you also apply for the "zero down" no payments for six months interest-free deals at several furniture stores. Each one of those credit applications will lower your credit score by five points or less, but if you have a borderline score, it will push you into a higher risk or a higher interest rate category.

> If you have always paid in cash and you've never taken out a loan for anything, it's possible to have a "0" credit score or what is referred to as a "no" or "thin file." Even if you have millions in the bank, you will still be treated as if you had bad credit or are just starting out. Why? They have no way to see what kind of risk you will be because they have no history to reference. In most cases, you will pay higher car, home, and renters insurance premiums.

Identity Theft

With all the data these credit reporting agencies and businesses have on you, it's inevitable at some point they will have a data breach. This could lead to your identity being stolen, commonly referred to as identity theft. This can cause serious issues for you short-term, long-term, or possibly for the rest of your life. A **credit freeze** is the best way to combat identity theft. You will need to **freeze your credit** with each of the major credit reporting agencies, not just one. When you freeze your credit, each of the credit reporting agencies will send you a special code that will be required to provide each time you want to access credit. Without the code, identity thieves can't open new lines of credit as if they were you, even if they have your other personal information. That brings up the question of, "If my credit is frozen, how am I able to grant access to those who may need to see it?" Great question!

Okay, imagine you want to buy a house and the mortgage company needs to pull your credit in order to approve the loan. First, you would need to find out which credit reporting agencies the lender uses to check your credit. Then you would need to **thaw** your credit with that credit reporting agency by using the special code they sent you previously. This is called "thawing your credit." It can be done as a temporary thaw for a specific amount of time, or it could be permanently thawed (not recommended).

Here are a few resources you can use to check your credit report and score.

1. AnnualCreditReport.com (Your credit report is free once a year from each of the credit reporting agencies).
2. Credit Karma or Credit Sesame (free credit scores). Your credit must not be frozen when enrolling, but can be frozen after you're enrolled.
3. Credit scores are available for free from your credit card company, and most of the time it is listed right on your monthly statement.
4. myFICO.com (You will need to pay to receive your credit score and report).

> There are other kinds of identity theft that you also need to be aware of such as, Medical, Synthetic, Insurance, Criminal, Driver's License, Social Security, and even Child Identity Theft. Be careful with your personal information and limit what you share and whom you share it with.

NUTSHELL

You are judged financially by what is on your credit report and how high of a credit score you have. With a lower score, you could face higher insurance rates, higher interest rates on loans, outright denials for credit, or denial of job offers. Know what's on your credit report by pulling a free copy from each of the three major credit reporting agencies (Equifax, Experian, and TransUnion) from AnnualCreditReport.com. Know what's on your credit report, and know your credit score and dispute any errors, so your credit reports reflect your true financial history.

Freezing your credit is one of the best ways to combat identity theft. Data breaches will continue to rise as companies put more and more value on knowing every detail of your life. They store and data mine every transaction, preference, like, dislike, and internet search. They want more and more of your personal information. That way, they can tailor their marketing specifically to you to maximize the chances you will buy from them and not someone else. It is very creepy how many intimate details these companies know about you and me. The worst part is when criminals get ahold of your data and start using it to open accounts as if they are you. That is where your trouble really begins. In a worst-case scenario, you could actually go to jail for someone else's actions because they pretended to be you. How scary is that?

CHAPTER 10

Planning to Win

(Budgeting & Financial Strategy)

MONEY HAS MAGIC-LIKE QUALITIES—if you're not paying attention, it will just disappear. By actively planning where and how you're spending your money, you'll know where your money is going and why. How can you keep your money from disappearing, you may ask. By having a spending plan in place, that's how! In other words, a budget and a financial strategy.

If you don't have or follow a financial road map, you can't expect your money to stick around. You'll continue to struggle and always wonder where your money went.

Have you ever used the phrase "I deserve it" or "I worked hard for it" to justify something you want to buy? Guess what? Life is not fair, and you don't deserve anything—you earn it! Let me repeat that for those of you who may have misunderstood my statement—you don't deserve anything; you earn it! If you truly deserve something, others will notice your work and tell you that you deserve it, or they will take action and reward you for your hard work and dedication.

The hardest part of a budget and a financial strategy is the actual commitment to staying within your budget and following the financial strategy that you've laid out, especially when issues arise or when really fun opportunities come along, but you don't have the money to address the issues or take part in the fun. Saying *no* now when you don't have the money will allow you to have more fun when you do have the money and achieve your financial success.

A budget and a financial strategy can sound complicated, restrictive, and even a bit scary for a number of reasons (no pun intended). First, you may not know how to create a budget. Second, you may feel your friends and family will judge you if they find out you are on a budget. Third, you may be scared to find out where you truly are financially. These are all very common concerns, and that's okay. You're doing something new and different and most likely something the people around you are not doing.

In order to move forward and achieve financial success, you need to know where you are financially. You may think you have a good idea of where you stand financially, but my guess is that you will be way off. That can be really scary, and no one can blame you for being scared. We have all had firsts in our lives. None of us got it right the first time, so don't stress out about it. You will learn how to create and use a budget, and over time, you'll get better and better at it. Has anyone ever explained to you why a budget and a financial strategy are so important or why they are such great tools to help you understand what's happening to your money, where it's going, and why you need each of these tools? I would guess that they haven't, and I would probably be right.

By having a budget and a financial strategy, you're able to see where you're at financially, what actions you need to take now, and where you can be financially in the future. You're also able to see the progress you're making and make any adjustments you may need to along the way, allowing you to meet your goal of being debt free and on your way to financial freedom.

For example, I'll assume you've traveled in a vehicle at some point in your life. Why do you use your GPS, and why are there signs along the road? They are there to help you go in the right

direction and get you to where you want to go. They only help you if you follow them, right? Well, guess what? A budget and a financial strategy will do the same thing. It's your road map. It's your GPS to get you where you want to go financially. That's it! That is all it is! If you can follow a road map or GPS, you can follow your budget and financial strategy, right?

Okay, okay already, enough jibber-jabber. Let's get you on your way and show you how to create a budget and a financial strategy so you can get started on your path to financial success!

Budget

What is a budget? A budget is a tool that helps you track your expenses, allowing you to control them before you get off course financially. In addition, it helps you plan for the week, month, and year ahead. It's a short-term plan for your money! That's it!

While there are several types of budgets, here are a few of the more common types: Zero-Based Budget, Static Budget, Flexible Budget, Incremental Budget, and the Rolling Budget.

I use a Zero-Based Budget (ZBB). It's easy to use and easy to understand, in my opinion. A Zero-Based Budget is what my wife and I have used for well over 10 years and what we will continue to use. The easiest way to track your spending is to get a receipt every time you spend any money. Then record those amounts daily in your budget. This will give you a real-time feel for what you are spending and where you're spending money.

I know, I know, (I can hear you already), it's just one more thing you have to do each day! Well, how important is your financial future to you? The reason you do this is to help you avoid problems later in the month because you are actively telling your money what to do and where to go. It's easy to do this earlier than later in the month. Right? Don't worry. After a few weeks, it will be your new normal. You can do this! You will want to do this to secure your financial future and to have a better life for yourself and your family.

With a Zero-Based Budget, you will assign a specific dollar amount to each line item within a category. This is to be completed before you start the month. Creating a budget before the month begins will help you keep on top of your spending, saving, and investment goals. A Zero-Based Budget takes about 2–4 months to get dialed in to where you will only need to make minor adjustments each month moving forward.

On page 61, you will see my version of a Zero-Based Budget. I used an Excel spreadsheet I've created, and it does most of the calculations for me. Obviously, it's a little difficult to see a spreadsheet in action in a printed book, but I will explain what happens.

For the most part, it's self-explanatory.

The "Household Income" is all the money coming in each month. This is recorded in the box to the right. This shows you how much is available to spend for the month.

If you have an income that is not consistent, such as commission-only income, where you have highs and lows through the year, then review your previous year's income and use the lowest amount received to calculate your household income. As larger paychecks come in, you can adjust your budget accordingly. During high-income months, you will want to save a portion of that "above normal" income to use during those dreaded low or no-income months. With little or no money coming in, it makes it very difficult meet your financial obligations, not to mention extremely stressful. By planning for those low or no-income months ahead of time, it will substantially reduce your stress and anxiety levels when you do have a low or no-income month.

The "Spend Plan" column is where you "spend" the household income on paper for any items that would apply for that month, such as groceries, gas, insurance, and so on. The amounts within the "Spend Plan" column are totaled to confirm the amount spent. That amount is noted in the box to the right of "Total Budget" column. Both the household income and the total budget should equal the same amount. This is confirmed by subtracting the "Total Budget" from the "Household Income." That amount is then noted in the box to the right

of "Balanced Budget." Zero (0) is what you should see each time you have completed your monthly Zero-Based Budget. However, it may show that you may need to adjust plus or minus a few items in the "Spend Plan" column in order to equal "0" for your Zero-Based Budget.

The "Weekly Total Spent" shows you how much you have spent each week by taking the amounts you have recorded within that week and providing you with a total. Why is this important? It's more insight into which weeks you are spending more money than other weeks and can help you plan better in the future.

The "Total Spent So Far This Month" is a running total of the money you're spending. This allows you to make adjustments to your budget earlier in the month rather than later, therefore avoiding any overspending.

The "Remaining Cash" is just that: your remaining cash for the month. This is calculated by subtracting the "Total Spent So Far This Month" from the "Household Income" each week and recording it in the correct week.

The "$Accum" or Accumulation column is used to record any money saved for particular line item (until it's needed), such as car insurance, vacations or gifts. For example, let's say your car insurance is $1,200 a year and is due in December. Being a smart money person, you decide to save $100 each month for 12 months. In January, you would save and record $100 in the $Accum column for the car insurance line item. In February, you would do the same but add the $100 from February to the existing $100 from January, for a total of $200 in the $Accum column at the end of February for the car insurance line item. You will end up doing this for multiple line items. There's also a box that shows the total amount you have accumulated just above the "$Accum" column for a quick reference. These amounts get carried from one month to the next and will change over time as you add to or subtract or use the accumulated money.

AUTO						$100.00	$0.00
BUDGETED ITEMS	SPEND PLAN	$ SPENT Week 1	$ SPENT Week 2	$ SPENT Week 3	$ SPENT Week 4	$ SPENT Week 5	$ ACCUM	DIFFERENCE
Vehicle Insurance	$100.00	-	-	$100.00	-	-	$100.00	-

The "Difference" column shows you the difference between what you had planned to spend and what you actually spent for each line item. This column shows whether you spent less than you planned or more than you planned on each specific line item. In reality, you may overspend in some areas and underspend in others.

Ideally, you will want to spend less than you planned to spend for each line item. This will allow you to have extra money to pay off a debt, save, or invest, depending on where you are in your journey to financial success. This is done by subtracting the total amounts spent for that line item from the "Spend Plan" amount of that line item. For example: You planned to spend $150 on electricity for the month, but when the bill comes, it's only for $125. Your budget would show in the Spend Plan column for the electricity line item as $150. You would then show the $125 in the "$SPENT Week" that you paid your bill, and in the "Difference" column, you would show the $25 of the money that was not used.

BUDGETED ITEMS	SPEND PLAN	$ SPENT Week 1	$ SPENT Week 2	$ SPENT Week 3	$ SPENT Week 4	$ SPENT Week 5	$ ACCUM	DIFFERENCE
UTILITIES							$0.00	$25.00
Electricity	$150.00	-	-	$125.00	-	-	$0.00	$25.00

The "Emergency Fund Running Total" shows the amount you have saved for your emergency fund. This amount is carried over from the Emergency Fund "$Accum" line item box until you meet your 3-, 6-, 9-, or 12-month emergency fund.

The items that are marked with "COO" (Cash Only Options) are to be paid with cash only. This will keep you from overspending when you can only buy with the cash you have. When it runs out, you cannot buy anything else! These are the areas in which overspending is way too easy to do when you use a debit or credit card. This normally happens with food, fun, and clothes!

The reason I want you to use cash is that you will make the connection between the physical cash in your wallet and how it emotionally affects you when you start to see your cash disappear. This jumpstarts the fight or flight response deep within your brain as you see a resource—money—disappear. You're going to fight to keep as much of that resource as you can. Then you will be able to focus on how that resource can best be used to your advantage instead of wasted.

HOUSEHOLD INCOME	
TOTAL BUDGET	
BALANCED BUDGET	
WEEKLY TOTAL SPENT	
REMAINING CASH	

TOTAL SPENT SO FAR THIS MONTH	

BUDGETED ITEMS	SPEND PLAN	$ SPENT Week 1	$ SPENT Week 2	$ SPENT Week 3	$ SPENT Week 4	$ SPENT Week 5	$ ACCUM	DIFFERENCE

EMERGENCY FUND RUNNING TOTAL			
3 Months	6 Months	9 Months	12 Months

COO = Cash Only Option

SAVING / INVESTING

Emergency Fund								
Savings								
Retirement Fund								
College Fund								
Investing								
Other								

HOUSING

1st Mortgage								
2nd Mortgage								
Property Tax								
Homeowner's / Renters Ins.								
Repairs / Maintenance								
Furnishings								
Other								

UTILITIES

Electricity								
Water								
Cell Phone								
Home Phone / Internet								
Trash								
Paid TV Service								
Other								
Other								

FOOD

Grocery (COO)								
Restaurants Family (COO)								
Restaurants Person 1 (COO)								
Restaurants Person 2 (COO)								
Other (COO)								
Other (COO)								

AUTO

Car Payment 1								
Car Payment 2								
Vehicle Insurance								
Gas / Oil (COO)								
Repairs / Tires / Maint. (COO)								
License / Taxes								
Vehicle Replacement								
Other								
Other								

CLOTHING

Adults (COO)								
Children (COO)								
Other (COO)								

MEDICAL / HEALTH

Health Ins / Doctor								
Dental Ins / Dentist								
Vision Ins / Optometrist								
Prescription / Vitamins								
Other (COO)								
Other (COO)								

PERSONAL

Life Insurance							
Disability Insurance							
Hair Care (COO)							
Toiletries / Cosmetics (COO)							
Gifts (Birthday / Christmas)							
School Tuition							
School Supplies							
Fun Time (COO)							
Donations (COO)							
Pet Care (COO)							
Other (COO)							
Other (COO)							

FUN STUFF

Entertainment (COO)							
Vacation							
Other (COO)							
Other (COO)							

DEBT | Debt Owed

Discover Card								
Master Card								
Visa								
American Express								
Dept. Store Card								
Other								
Other								
Other								
Other								
Other								

Head over to DirkWrites.com and sign up for the Inside Scoop! Receive a FREE copy of this budget and a BONUS resource. Only those who sign up will find out what the BONUS is and how it can help you with a huge financial decision.

Here is an example:

HOUSEHOLD INCOME	$2,000.00					
TOTAL BUDGET	$2,000.00		TOTAL SPENT SO FAR THIS MONTH		$1,813.80	
BALANCED BUDGET	$0.00					
WEEKLY TOTAL SPENT		$969.36	$150.55	$487.08	$166.81	$40.00
REMAINING CASH		$1,030.64	$880.09	$393.01	$226.20	$186.20

							$255.00	$62.45
BUDGETED ITEMS	SPEND PLAN	$ SPENT Week 1	$ SPENT Week 2	$ SPENT Week 3	$ SPENT Week 4	$ SPENT Week 5	$ ACCUM	DIFFERENCE

EMERGENCY FUND RUNNING TOTAL			
3 Months	6 Months	9 Months	12 Months
$500.00	-	-	-

COO = Cash Only Option

HOUSING

1st Mortgage	$500.00	$500.00	-	-	-	-	-	$0.00
2nd Mortgage	$142.41	-	-	$142.41	-	-	-	-
Property Tax	$200.00	-	-	-	$126.25	-	$200.00	-
Homeowner's / Renters Ins.	$55.00	-	-	$55.00	-	-	$55.00	-

UTILITIES

Electricity	$150.00	$200.00	-	-	-	-	-	($50.00)
Water	$30.00	-	$21.81	-	-	-	-	$8.19
Cell Phone	$75.00	-	$75.00	-	-	-	-	-
Home Phone / Internet	$52.59	-	-	$52.59	-	-	-	-

FOOD

Grocery (COO)	$300.00	$152.01	$2.34	$107.05	-	-	-	$38.60
Restaurants Family (COO)	$200.00	$27.35	$21.40	$50.03	$15.56	-	-	$85.66
Restaurants Person 1 (COO)	$170.00	$80.00	$10.00	$50.00	-	$40.00	-	($10.00)
Restaurants Person 2 (COO)	$75.00	$10.00	$20.00	$30.00	$25.00	-	-	($10.00)
Other (COO)	$50.00	-	-	-	-	-	-	$0.00

Take your time when setting up your budget for the first time. Understand where you need to spend and where you want to spend your money. Record your spending daily. Review your actual spending against where you had planned to spend your money weekly. Really look at *what* you're spending money on and *where* you're spending your money. Make adjustments early in the month to stay on track! A team effort can really keep you on track—make sure as a family you are on board and working together toward the same goal. This will be challenging from time to time, but when you are *not* living paycheck to paycheck, you will see why it *is* worth doing. Communication is the key to your financial future. Now that you have your budget worked out, let's work on your financial strategy.

> *Dirk says . . .*
> ## WHEN I KNOW ENOUGH TO KNOW I DON'T KNOW ENOUGH, I START ASKING QUESTIONS.

Financial Strategy

What is a financial strategy? It's a plan to reach your financial goals. That's it! Sounds kind of simple, right? It would be if life stayed the same, but that's not exactly how life works.

You will need to figure what your short-term and long-term visions of financial success look like to create your financial strategy. Your financial strategy will be different from someone else's. Why, you may ask. It all depends on where you're starting from financially and at *what* stage of life you are at. Someone just starting their working career will have a vastly different financial strategy than someone who is about to retire. That's why creating and following a budget is such an important part of your financial strategy.

A successful financial strategy needs to have a set of guidelines in place before getting started. These guidelines will help you stay between the lines, so to speak, and help you make better financial decisions moving forward. This is especially important when emotions and peer pressure come into play.

1. **Financial awareness is #1. Being financially aware is understanding that almost everything you do will have some kind of financial impact on your budget.**

   An example would be driving to the store to buy groceries. The obvious focus would be on the cost of the groceries; however, the transportation cost needs to be included, but it is often overlooked because that specific trip cost is a very, very small fraction of the whole cost and determining it is not worth the time and effort to do so. That being said, many other costs are also overlooked that are part of the drive to buy groceries, including the vehicle itself, gas, oil, tires, vehicle maintenance, insurance, driver's license, tags, and taxes. I bet you didn't think such a common task as going to buy groceries involved so many other items and created such a financial impact to your wallet. Did you?

2. **Know the percentages on how much you should be spending in a given category.**

   Typically, categories are broken down as follows:

   - Food (7–15%)
   - Housing (20–28%)
   - Utilities (5–10%)
   - Transportation (10%–15%)
   - Clothing (5%)
   - Savings (10–15%)
   - Medical (5–10%)
   - Personal (5–10%)
   - Entertainment (5–10%)
   - Debt (0–10%)
   - Giving (0–15%)

Make sure your budget is in line with these percentages. These are recommended percentages. How high or low your take-home pay is will highly affect the percentages needed for the necessities.

3. Research before you buy. Be in the know. Do not impulse buy.

4. Avoid or step away from situations involving high pressure or high emotions when you're making a financial decision. You will most likely make a different choice when you have a chance to run the numbers yourself and understand what impact that decision will have on you financially.

Now that you have your budget set up, let's get started with a financial strategy that gives you breathing room before you start eliminating your debt. This way, when you have an issue that requires that something be fixed immediately, you have cash on hand to fix it.

Starter Emergency Fund

First, you want to create a little buffer with a starter emergency fund. I recommend $500–$600 for individuals and $1,000–$1,100 for a family. Just put it in a savings account for now, in case you really need it for a *true* emergency, such as an unexpected car repair. This is just a starter emergency fund—in case something happens, you have cash to pay for it.

In the event you need to use some or all of your starter emergency fund, you will need to replace the money before continuing to eliminate debt. Later, you will build a 6–9-month emergency fund after you pay off your debt.

Okay, let's move on to a financial strategy that gets you out of debt.

Debt Elimination

There are several common opinions on how you should best attack your debt. Some say doing a consolidation loan is the best way to pay off your debt. Others say paying off the highest interest rates first is the best way, and yet others say paying off your debts from smallest to largest is the best way. There are also opinions in between. Let's dig into this a little to see what some of the pros and cons are.

Taking out a debt-consolidation loan

Pros:

- You have only one payment to make each month.
- There is just one interest rate to deal with.

Cons:

- With one large amount to pay off, little traction is noticed.
- Credit is available on other cards (as well as the temptation to use it).
- Your money habits and/or mindset may not change.

From a commonsense standpoint, this sounds like it should work out the best, but studies show this is the least effective way to eliminate debt. Most people do not change their spending habits and end up back where they started or worse, go deeper in debt, with this approach.

Paying off the highest interest rates first

Pros:

- You will save on the amount of interest you pay out.

Cons:

- You could have a high interest rate with a high balance leaving a smaller balance that could have been paid off.
- The balance may not go down as fast.
- You may not see progress being made and give up before too long.
- Your money habits and/or mindset may not change.

By far this is the most recommended way and mathematically the most efficient way to eliminate your debt. However, *this doesn't take into account our emotional needs in this process.* You are trying to change your mindset on how you use money, and in most cases, you are looking at larger amounts to pay off before you see progress, and you experience fewer wins up front. Having more wins would build your stamina.

> ## Dirk says . . .
>
> ## WHAT IS YOUR FUTURE WORTH TO YOU?
> ## WHAT ARE YOU WILLING TO SACRIFICE
> ## TO HAVE A BETTER FUTURE?

Paying off the lowest balance first

Pros:

- You will see real progress with eliminating your debt.

Cons:

- You pay more out on interest.
- Your money habits and/or mindset may not change.

This approach gets you several wins in short order. You're able to see the traction you're making, which builds your confidence and stamina along the way, so when you get to your larger debt amounts, you have more money to throw at the debt. Second but most importantly, you have a proven track record that you can do this! This is mathematically a slightly less efficient way to eliminate debt, but the success rates far outweigh the other two approaches as studies have shown.

> None of these options will work if you don't change your mindset and change how you use money! That being said, you will need to define what your financial goals are first, so you can put a financial strategy in place to obtain your goals. If you're in debt, your first goal should be to stop going any deeper into debt. Your second goal should be getting out of debt.

Debt Elimination Plan

I would suggest the "Paying off the lowest balance first" option to get yourself out of debt, knowing that this method has a greater success rate than the others. Start with listing your debts from smallest to largest. The highest priority is given to those bills that are not current, especially back taxes (IRS) or a home foreclosure. If everything is current, you will want to pay the minimums on all of your debts except the lowest balance. You will want to use all your remaining money toward that one to eliminate that debt. Then repeat the process for each remaining debt.

Top 9 ways to speed up your process of getting out of debt

1. Get another job or two or three.
2. Sell your unused household items.
3. Sell your unused vehicle or recreational vehicles.
4. Sell your vehicle that you shouldn't have bought in the first place to get rid of the payment that is crushing you every month.
5. Sell your vehicle if you have more than a 42-month (3½ years) loan on it. You're paying way too much in interest over the life of the loan and are more likely to default on the loan because you're most likely strapped financially already. That's why you needed to take out a longer-term loan in the first place.
6. If the total amount owed on your vehicles combined is 50% or more of your take-home pay, you need to sell, sell, sell! This is too much of a drain on you financially.
7. Sell that rental or vacation home that you have another mortgage on. You can always buy another one when you are out of debt and can actually pay cash for it.
8. In some cases, you may want to sell your house to get out of debt and wipe the slate clean.
9. Start a micro-business with the skills you have with zero or a very low startup cost to generate more income.

NUTSHELL

To reach financial success, you need to have a plan and guidelines in place. This allows you to follow that plan. A budget is a tool; a financial strategy is the plan that will help you reach your financial goals. You are planning ahead by using a Zero-Based Budget. You're telling your money where it's going to go instead of waiting until the end of the month to figure out where your money went.

CHAPTER 11

Quick and Easy Financial Wins

YOU ARE CONTINUOUSLY PUSHED to sign up to receive your bills online and sign up for automatic payments so "you will never miss a payment." Set it and forget it! That's right, you *will* forget about it, and that's the whole idea behind auto pay. Companies are betting that you won't check your monthly billing statements after you've signed up for auto pay. This all but guarantees they'll be able to raise your rates with little or no push back, as you're more likely to not review your bills every month. Typically, autopay is used for bills such as home/cell phone, internet, paid TV, lawn care, laundry service, or any other monthly bills you can sign up for.

Quick financial wins are both quick and easy—all it takes is a phone call. It's really that simple! Look at your cable bill, gasp, "That's how much I've been paying," pick up the phone, call your service provider, and tell

them your bill is too high and that you're looking for them to lower your bill, but you want to keep the same service. If "customer no service" tells you that there's nothing that they can do, ask them to transfer you to the Customer Retention Department. Why? Well, it costs more money for them to get a new customer than it does to keep an existing customer. Don't be afraid to change service providers if they don't reduce your bill. Remember it is your money, so why not keep as much of it as you can?

You will also need to review your car/renters or home insurances as well. These bills are *not* normally billed monthly but are often forgotten about until you get the bill. Make sure you shop around for better coverage at a lower cost. Also take a look at your auto-renewal contracts such as gym memberships, cell phone plans, online services, and so on.

Review where you're banking and what kind of fees they charge you for the services you use. Do you have overdraft protection on your checking account? This is pitched as a service that will save you from missing a payment or having an embarrassing moment when your transaction is declined, but in fact, this is a money maker for the bank or credit union. For each transaction that is covered by the overdraft protection, you're charged around $30.

They actually have software that calculates which combination of your transactions will maximize *their* number of overdraft protection charges and will process the transaction in that sequence, not in the order they were charged. How does that make you feel? If you remove the overdraft protection from your account, when you have a $0.00 balance, the debit card transaction is denied at no charge. That seems like a much better deal to me. What do you think? However, if you are still using checks, you may want to keep it in place, as it is a crime to write a check from an account that has insufficient funds available.

Look at changing to a credit union, where you're technically an owner, meaning you will be getting lower rates on loans and higher rates on savings. Plus, there may be other advantages that your local credit union can offer that will fit your needs perfectly.

NUTSHELL

Pick up the phone and ask for a discount on your bills. If you don't ask, you won't know. It's your money. Why not keep more of it?

CHAPTER 12

I'll Pay for That Later!
(Credit Cards)

DANGER! DANGER! DANGER! DANGER! DANGER! DANGER! DANGER! DANGER! DANGER! DANGER!

HERE'S SOMETHING TO THINK about. If cash is king, why do you use plastic? Wow, that is a great question, if I do say so myself. Hopefully, you got the hint from the banner above that credit cards can be dangerous to your financial success. Over time, credit cards have been woven into the fabric of our everyday lives. This first started back in 1951, when the first credit cards were issued. Slowly over the years, it has become common practice to use a credit card for everyday purchases such as gas, food, clothing, vacations, and so on, but unfortunately *"common practice does not equal common sense."* The push has always been that it's a way to build your credit and show how responsible you are with money.

That's not it at all, though. It actually shows if you're responsible at *paying back the money you borrowed*. If you were responsible with money, you would not need a credit card in the first place. You would have money in the bank. Since 1951, we have been conditioned to feel that it's "okay" and "normal" to buy something now and pay for it later. The problem comes when the "later" arrives and it's time to pay up.

What's the problem? Well, the problem is you're overspending and unable to pay your bill in full. Why is this a problem? This can be the start of a downward financial spiral that's very easy to get caught up in and very difficult to get out of.

A credit card is a form of an unsecured *loan*—that's right, a *loan*. Meaning, it comes with terms and conditions that you're agreeing to when you use their credit card, but you already know that because you've read the terms and conditions when you applied for the credit card. Right? But truly, how many people have actually read the terms and conditions of a credit card application before they signed it? Did you? All we hear or see when applying for a credit card is sign here, here, initial here, sign and date here, and you're good to go. Sound familiar? Yeah, I thought so. Then, if you're approved, you'll receive your credit card within 7–10 business days along with your approved credit limit.

Credit limit—what's that? This is the amount that the credit card company feels safe lending you based on their risk assessment of you, your credit background check, financial payment history, income, and current financial obligations. What it comes down to is whether you are worthy to carry a piece of plastic with their logo on it.

Take a look at this and see if this makes financial sense to you and your wallet.

Say your take-home pay is $3,000 a month, and your expenses are $2,800 a month, leaving you with $200 surplus each month. You're feeling like a responsible adult, so you apply and are approved for a credit card with a $5,000 credit limit.

Before the credit card, you only had $200 that you could spend each month.

After the credit card approval and for at least the first month, you could spend up to $5,200.

If you maxed out the card in the first month, it would take you over 2 years to pay off the credit card using all of the $200 surplus every month while never using the card again. This doesn't include any of the interest that would need to be paid for taking out that loan!

What are the chances that you're not going to use the card again at any point while you're trying to pay off the balance? I would say kind of slim. It's unlikely you would be willing to sacrifice for that long without using the card again.

Now, imagine you only charge $600 on the card. It will take you 3 months to pay off the card in full (interest not included) using all of your $200 surplus every month.

What are the chances here that you're not going to use the card again at any point while you're trying to pay off that balance? I'd say even slimmer. It's unlikely that you would be willing to sacrifice for 3 months and use all of your surplus. You are more likely to spread out paying that $600 off over six months, so that way you still have surplus cash each month. It's only a little interest that you'll be paying, and that's okay, right? Then other things pop up, and you keep reaching for the credit card because it's there, it's convenient, and you can always pay it off later. Right?

When you see it laid out clearly, you see that it doesn't make financial sense for you or your wallet.

Dirk says . . .
IF CASH IS KING,
WHY DO YOU USE PLASTIC?

Now let's scale this up and take a look at how well this credit card idea is working for the vast majority of Americans. As always, it depends on which news channel or expert you're listening to, but Americans are carrying over **1 TRILLION DOLLARS** in credit card debt alone! That's right, you read that correctly: over **1 TRILLION DOLLARS** in credit card debt.

That should jolt you out of that little fairy tale you're trying to sell yourself on and how having a credit card is no big deal. The chances are overwhelming that you will end up carrying a balance on one or more of your credit cards. You'll become another statistic just like all those other people who said, "It can't happen to me. I'll never carry a balance." This is the reality, and it's backed up by a whole lot of data from a whole lot of sources.

Credit card debt can be a dark cloud in your life, always there, always restricting you and preventing you from doing better financially—and the credit card company is okay with that. You are their little profit center, and they want you to stay right where you're at, never paying your balance in full. As long as you keep paying them each month, they'll keep lending you money month after month after month. Besides, who else are they going to get to pay for their corporate jets, private country club memberships, and private yachts? Isn't it nice to know you're helping others build their dreams and fund their financial goals?

Oftentimes people look at credit cards as free money, just like one of those gift cards or stored value cards, especially those who have never had a credit card before, such as college students or young adults. They don't realize that at some point, the money they were *loaned* will have to be paid back with interest. Remember—these are loans that you're taking out each time you swipe that card.

You will receive a statement from the credit card company letting you know how much money you owe them based on the charges you made in the previous billing cycle. To make things even more interesting, the credit card statements themselves can be confusing as they have different acronyms and/or phrases, such as APR (annual percentage rate), variable rate, daily balance method (including new transactions), average daily balance method, daily periodic rate (DPR), interest rate or a nominal interest rate, annual percentage yield, effective annual rate, and many others that you need to understand before you start using your credit card and especially if you are going to carry a balance.

There are two types of APRs. One is a fixed APR, and the other is a variable APR. A fixed APR will not change but in most cases is not guaranteed to never change. A variable APR can change on a regular basis, but in both cases, you will be notified of the change before it takes effect. There may be additional factors in play based on the user agreement, such as specific fees for specific transitions.

The interest on your credit card balance is compounded daily! That's right. Daily, on unpaid balances. Are you starting to see why it doesn't take long to go deeper and deeper in debt if you're only paying the minimum and continue to use your credit card? If you want to figure out how much interest you're going to be paying on your unpaid balance, it's going to take a little math to get to that information.

It's actually a four-step process to determine how much interest you're going to pay on an unpaid balance. That's just crazy! Shouldn't this be easier to figure this out? Yep, it could be, but then you'd be shocked at how much you're paying and probably want to stop carrying a balance. That would be bad for the credit card company, so they purposely make it time-consuming and difficult to figure out.

Let's walk through the four steps.

1. First, find the APR listed on your statement. We will use 12% for this example.

2. Divide the APR by 365 (days in a year) to get your daily periodic rate (DPR). Credit cards charge interest *daily*, not annually, on an unpaid balance that is carried over to the next billing cycle.
   - 12% (APR) ÷ 365 (days per year) = .00032 (DPR)

3. Calculate your average daily balance (ADB) over a billing cycle. We're going to use a 30-day billing cycle for this example. Say you start November 1 with an $1,800 unpaid balance from the previous billing cycle. Then on November 16, you make an $800 payment, leaving an unpaid balance of $1,000 for the remainder of the billing cycle ending on November 30. You will need to add up each of the daily balances for the entire billing cycle to find the sum of your daily balances.
   - $1,800 × 15 Days = $27,000 (ADB)
   - $1,000 × 15 Days = $15,000 (ADB)
   - $27,000 + $15,000 = $42,000 (SUM of daily balances)
   - $42,000 ÷ 30 Days = $1,400 (ADB) for the month

4. Calculate what the interest will be by using the Average Daily Balance × Daily Periodic Rate × Days in the billing cycle.
   - $1,400 (ADB) × .00032 (DPR) × 30 Days = $13.44 of interest

You will be charged $13.44 of interest on that unpaid balance. However, because interest is calculated daily, your balance will continue to rise every day until a payment is made or the balance is paid off.

The reality is that you probably have or are going to have a credit card at some point. I get that. The key is to not charge what you do not have. It is a really simple concept to understand, but a very difficult one to implement in real life, especially when life happens. But trust me, it is *not worth* all the headaches that you're going to cause yourself.

Dirk says . . .

LIFE IS A SERIES OF TRADE-OFFS. YOU TRADE YOUR TIME FOR MONEY. YOU TRADE YOUR MONEY FOR THINGS. ARE YOU TRADING YOUR FUTURE FOR THE PRESENT, WHEN YOU SHOULD BE TRADING YOUR PRESENT FOR YOUR FUTURE?

I would be remiss if I did not mention department store credit cards. These cards can only be used in that specific department store chain. These cards are not a good way to build credit if that's what you're looking to do. Normally they offer a discount in order to get you to sign up and then run promotions to get you to use your card, hoping you will overspend and carry a balance.

This is not to be confused with store-branded credit cards that are in fact true credit cards and can be used anywhere. Store-branded cards typically provide a reward for using that specific card that aligns with your interests such as cruising, electronics, hardware stores, and so on.

> A credit card company can lower your credit limit at any time or cancel your card altogether. If this happens, your credit score will be affected and can cause a ripple effect on the ratios that show your credit usage versus your credit availability. You can lower this risk by having two different credit cards issued by two different financial institutions, such as having one issued from a bank and the other issued from a credit union.

I am not promoting the use of credit cards but merely giving information on how the game is played. To keep the card active, you do need to make a small charge under $2 twice a year or the credit card company can cancel the card for non-use.

Always avoid those 0% interest for X number of months! In the fine print of the contract, you will find a gotcha! If you don't follow the contract down to the letter, all that interest that you were avoiding, well, you're now going to pay it and probably more. So that toaster oven wasn't a great deal after all.

NUTSHELL

It's really simple—don't charge more than you have in the bank. There will always be hiccups in life, but don't compound them by making poor financial decisions that will haunt you for years. Self-control and discipline are two characteristics that you must have if you're planning on having and using a credit card. Without them, you will end up like most of the people around you: all flash, no cash, living from paycheck to paycheck month after month, year after year, always struggling to make ends meet, always wondering why you can't get ahead. You can also look forward to being stressed out for months, years, or even decades. That doesn't sound like much fun, does it?

Not carrying a balance will save you a lot of money. Frequently making payments to your credit card will also save you money. I recommend paying off your credit card weekly or at least making payments weekly to lower the balance and lower the amount of interest that is accruing. This helps you track how much and what you're spending your money on. Knowing your own spending habits and triggers will help you avoid impulse buying and overspending. If you always overspend when you buy clothes, leave your credit card at home and bring only the amount of cash you're willing to spend. This will force you to only spend what you have, or even spend less.

CHAPTER 13

I Can't Drive 55!

(Car Insurance and Buying That New Ride)

A SURPRISING COST THAT IS normally an afterthought is car insurance. This book is a little different. I want to challenge you to think differently about your financial decisions. That's why you need to look at car insurance *before* you buy a car, not after. Research how much the insurance is going to cost you as well as which kinds of coverages you will need for the type of vehicle your thinking about buying. In most cases, you're going to be surprised and not in a good way at how much it's going to cost you to insure your dream vehicle. By looking at your insurance costs first, you may change your mind on which kind of vehicle you're going to buy. I can't imagine how much money I could have saved if I would have known about this little life hack before I bought my first car.

Keeping That Ride Safe

Once you have decided on the type of vehicle, you need to shop around for insurance and get a minimum of *three* quotes. Make sure each of the quotes has the same coverage. By doing this, you will get the best price and the best coverage. Keep in mind that not all insurance companies are created equal, and the lowest price is not always the best option. You will need to look at the ratings of the insurance company as well as the reviews they receive regarding the overall customer experience. All insurance companies are graded by AM Best. Look for insurance companies that have an AM Best grade of A or higher.

Comparing the insurance cost will enlighten you on how much difference there can be from one car to the next. For example, compare insuring a Dodge Charger versus a Dodge Viper or insuring a Ford Focus versus a Ford Mustang. There's a huge difference between the Charger and Viper, as well as a huge difference between the Focus and Mustang, and even between the Charger and Focus and the Viper and the Mustang. The type of car you choose will have a direct impact on your wallet.

> If you already have insurance, you still need to shop for new insurance at least every 2 years, especially if your rates go up and you haven't had an accident. Your vehicle is going down in value, so the cost to insure the vehicle should also go down.

Okay, let's dial it back and review some of the basics of insurance so you have a better understanding of insurance and what it covers.

What is insurance?

The *Oxford Dictionary* defines insurance as "An arrangement by which a company or the state undertakes to provide a guarantee of compensation for specified loss, damage, illness, or death in return for payment of a specified premium."

In other words, you're transferring some of your financial risk to someone else by paying them a set amount of money at prearranged times. The company or state will pay for covered losses.

What is an insurance premium?

The premium is an amount to be paid to the insurance company or state at prearranged times for a contract of insurance.

What is a deductible?

The *Oxford Dictionary* defines a deductible as "The part of an insurance claim to be paid by the insured; an excess."

In other words, you will need to pay out of pocket a set amount that is stated in your insurance contract or policy before the insurance company will pay anything.

Dirk says . . .

MONEY IS A TOOL WE USE TO BUY PEOPLE'S TIME TO DO SOMETHING WE CAN'T DO, DON'T WANT TO DO, DON'T KNOW HOW TO DO, OR DON'T HAVE ENOUGH TIME TO DO.

Common Types of Vehicle Insurance

Bodily Injury Liability

This coverage pays for pain and suffering, lost wages or income, medical bills, and funeral expenses in an accident where you were at fault. This also pays for legal costs to defend you in a lawsuit as a result of the accident.

Property Damage Liability

If you are at fault, you are responsible for the repairs to another person's vehicle or property. Property damage coverage also includes anything hit with your vehicle, such as a fence, house, parking meter, or street light.

Collision

In most cases, if your vehicle is financed, you will be required to have this coverage. This type of coverage pays for damage to your car if you have a collision with another vehicle. If you are at fault, you will be reimbursed for the cost of repairs once your deductible has been paid. If the other driver is at fault, your insurance company will seek reimbursement from the other driver's insurance company for the cost of your repairs.

Comprehensive

Usually, if your vehicle is financed, you will be required to have this coverage. This type of coverage protects you from losses that include vandalism, theft, fires, falling objects, earthquakes, storms, or damage due to hitting an animal.

Uninsured and Underinsured Motorist Coverage

There are two types of uninsured and underinsured motorist coverage available: bodily injury coverage and property damage coverage. You can choose one or the other or both depending on your specific needs. This type of coverage can protect you, passengers in your vehicle, and your vehicle if you are injured in an accident by an underinsured or uninsured motorist and they are held responsible for your injuries. This coverage pays for medical expenses or related expenses that you have incurred up to your policy limits.

Gap Insurance

This type of coverage is optional, but it may be needed if you owe more on your vehicle than it is worth. It covers the "gap" between the two so that your vehicle is fully covered.

Example costs and coverage

Here is an example of what you could see for costs and coverage in an insurance policy.

You may have a $1,200 a year premium with a $500 deductible (but not if you are a teenager or have a sports car).

The insurance policy coverage could be similar to the below:

A. **Liability**
  - Bodily injury:
    - » Each person $250,000
    - » Each accident $500,000
  - Property damage: each accident $100,000

B. **Medical payments: each person $5,000**

C. **Uninsured motorists: each person $100,000**
  - Bodily injury: each accident $300,000
  - Property damage: each accident $50,000

D. **Damage to your vehicle**
  - Collision loss:
    - » Actual Cash Value (ACV) minus deductible
  - Other-than-collision loss:
    - » Actual Cash Value (ACV) minus deductible

The insurance company has the obligation to cover up to a specific amount stated in the insurance policy once you have paid your deductible.

If you were to have an accident and the damages were less than $500, your insurance company would not cover the damages because you would not have met your deductible.

If you were to have an accident and the damages were to exceed your $500 deductible, you would first need to pay the $500 deductible to your insurance company before the insurance company would cover the damages that exceeded your deductible. Let's say the accident caused $25,000 in damages. You would pay out of your pocket $500 (your deductible) to your insurance company. That would leave $24,500 that would be covered by the insurance company in most cases, depending on the coverages you have chosen or listed in your policy.

> Car insurance requirements vary by state and can differ if you have a loan
> on your vehicle, so check with your state to find out more.

How can you keep your premiums low?

Well, you can raise your deductible (out of pocket) from $500 to $750 or $1,000 or even higher if you can afford it. The higher the deductible, the lower your premium. Make sure you have your deductible set aside in your emergency fund in the event you have to pay your deductible. You can also lower the coverage amounts to lower your premium, or you can do both to get even a lower premium.

Another way to keep your premiums low is *not* to file small claims with your insurance, such as a chipped windshield or door dents. You may opt to pay for the repairs out of pocket to avoid a rise in your premiums in the future. It may hurt your wallet at first, but at least you will not be hit with higher premiums for years and years to come.

Note

This is not legal or insurance advice, and you will need to determine the best course of action for yourself.

Dirk says . . .

WHAT ARE YOU WILLING TO PAY WITH—YOUR TIME OR YOUR MONEY—TO GET YOU FROM WHERE YOU ARE NOW TO WHERE YOU WANT TO BE?

Now that you understand some of the basics of car insurance, what it covers, and how choosing the correct vehicle can help you financially, you can apply this knowledge to get the best coverage at the best rate.

Buying That New Ride

Buying New

Do you smell it? No? Take a deep breath. Ahhhh, there it is, that new car smell! You've got to love it! Yeah, that nice, new shiny ride you're about to drive off the lot . . . **DON'T!** Well, at least not until you read this chapter.

First off, **vehicles go down in value.** Knowing this up front will help you understand that a vehicle is *not* an investment. You're also buying the second most expensive item in your life. And, oh yeah, did I mention it *goes down in value*? Second, buy a vehicle with cash! Why? This will force you to buy what you can truly afford, not what other people say you can afford. It goes back to your mindset.

> ▌ We are not talking about classic cars here that could increase in value.

Run the numbers on buying a new vehicle and see if you're making the right financial decision.

- The average new vehicle price is around $34,077.
- The average length of a car loan is 65 months or 5.42 years.
- The average interest rate by average loan term is 3.855%.
- Finally, the average monthly car payment is $524.26.

Here's what happens financially when you buy that shiny new vehicle. I'll put some numbers to it so you will have a better picture of what's happening. I'm going to use the average new vehicle price of $34,077. You may or may not know this, but as soon as you drive a vehicle off the lot, that vehicle is no longer worth what you paid for it. Well, that is a bad deal even if you got a good deal on the vehicle.

You will lose approximately 10% of the value of the vehicle just signing those papers and driving off into the sunset. Wow, just like that, you lost $3,407.70 in value! Your shiny new vehicle is now only worth $30,669.30, and that is not all the bad news. By the end of the first year, your vehicle will lose an additional 10% of its value, so now your slightly used vehicle has lost a total of $6,815.40 in value and is now only worth $27,261.60. However, depending

---

on the make and model, your new vehicle could lose as much as 50% of its value in the first year. On average, a new vehicle will lose at least 60% of its value over the first 5 years. This means in 5 years or less, your vehicle will have **lost $20,446.20** in value, meaning its now only worth $13,630.80. **Take a good look at this— you took $34,077 and turned it into $13,630.80 in 5 years or less.** This is not how to obtain financial success! You are going in the wrong direction! Would you agree?

All that being said, it does not account for *the emotional want* of a new vehicle! I get it, I really do. This is a real factor you will need to deal with when you are making big and small financial decisions. However, this is not overlooked in the financial world. In fact, your emotions are targeted to get you to spend your money or, more to the point, someone else's money. We are bombarded constantly with marketing/ads/social media showing how, "You too can afford a new vehicle at a low, low monthly payment." Lower payments over a longer period of time means more of your money will be going into their pockets. They don't have to live your life, and they don't have to pay your bills. They just want to add to them. You have to be financially aware of how you're spending your money.

Is it a need or a want? If it is a need, not a problem, but *do not* try to upgrade your need into a want. Consider this example. You need transportation. You can buy a nice used car for $15,000 cash, but once you start looking at cars and talking to the dreaded used car guy or gal, you start looking at new cars that are around $25,000. You start thinking, *Well, if I buy a new car, it has a warranty, and I won't have to worry about it for a long time. Whereas with a used car, well, it's used, and you don't know what kind of issues it's had in the past.* See how quickly you can justify making a poor financial decision?

Assuming that you need transportation, you should look at public transportation as your first option, if it is available in your area. If that is not available, consider buying a dependable older used vehicle. Both of these would fit the "need" category and would get you to and from your destinations. Anything more than this and you would be upgrading to the "want" category. I know that is hard to hear, but it is the truth.

WARNING!

You will also try to justify and make up all kinds of reasons you need to upgrade to your "want," but don't do it.

> You may not be taking into account alternate forms of transportation, such as walking, biking, ride sharing, or taking a car service. These are all viable options that can save you a lot of money over time, giving you the opportunity to invest more and sooner than you expected.

If you do decide to take out a car loan, you must read all of the loan documents in their entirety. Know the details of what you are signing before you sign any legal document or contract. Not knowing the details can cost you money. I bring this up as there are still lenders out there who calculate the loan's interest using the sum of digits, better known as the Rule of 78s. This is an old trick that benefits the lender because it frontloads the interest. Even if you pay off your loan early, you're paying more interest than if you had a simple-interest car loan.

Buying Used

Buying a used vehicle is your next and best option (unless of course someone gives you a vehicle). Plain and simple, buying a used vehicle will save you a lot of money! As you can see from above, *the value of a new vehicle drops significantly over 5 years*. Buying a used vehicle eliminates a lot of that loss and will keep more money in your pocket. The great news is that vehicle reliability has improved dramatically over the years, and vehicles are on the road a lot longer than they used to be.

This should give you the confidence to buy an older vehicle. As noted above, pay cash for your vehicle. This will force you to buy only that which you can truly afford. Start out by buying a dependable older used vehicle 10–20 years old at first. Then adjust your budget and set aside money each month so you will be able to save up, trade-in/sell and move up to a newer used vehicle. Continue to do this until you're able to buy a newer used vehicle between 3–5 years old. This will get you the best value for a newer used vehicle while letting someone else take the loss in value. Depending on the type and age of the used vehicle, you can expect to pay anywhere from $23,000 down to as low as $500 for a vehicle that is between 3–20 years old.

Dirk says . . .

IF YOU'RE IN DEBT, YOU'RE TRADING FUTURE OPPORTUNITIES FOR FEEL-GOOD MOMENTS RIGHT NOW.

Lease a Vehicle

Can I lease a vehicle as an option? In a word, *no*. Leasing is basically renting, and you're paying a premium to do this. You will have all of the responsibility and obligations with none of the benefits. You're required to insure and maintain the vehicle, and you are also restricted on the number of miles you can drive during the term of your lease. If you go over the mileage allowance, you will have to pay a penalty for every mile over that allowance. Conversely, they do not pay you for the unused miles, and in the end, you spend a lot of money and have nothing to show for it because you turn the car back in at the end of your lease. But if you bought the vehicle outright, you still have the vehicle.

Do Your Research

Is the used vehicle worth what they're asking? Check out NADA.com, KBB.com, Edmunds.com, or CarGurus.com to get a feel for the price of the vehicle. Make sure to check the VIN (vehicle identification number)! Use CarFax.com to check if the vehicle has been in a major accident or flood. Also, check out ConsumerReports.org or JDPower.com for ratings and reliability for the vehicle that you are looking to purchase.

Test Drive

Test driving is a must before you buy any vehicle. All the research and features are not going to do you any good if you are not happy with how the vehicle performs or feels to you. Remember, you will be using it every day for the next 5 to 10 years, so you need to make sure you really like it.

Vehicle Inspection

Stipulate that you will need to have the vehicle inspected by an independent mechanic of your choosing before you sign any paperwork. When you buy a used car, you buy it "as-is," and it *does not matter what the sales person tells you*. You can check CarFax, but that is not enough; you need to take this additional step to ensure you're getting a reliable vehicle that is not going to cause you issues later on.

Dirk says . . .

SOME PEOPLE ARE "ALL FLASH AND NO CASH."

Pay with CASH

If you don't have the cash to buy a vehicle, you cannot buy the vehicle! Why? You are on a budget, and the interest you would be paying out to service the loan is better spent on eliminating your debt.

Alright, you now have the knowledge and the tools, and it is up to you to make the right financial decision when buying your vehicle.

> Just to clarify, I'm not saying you can never by a new vehicle, but you need to reach a level of financial success in order to absorb the loss in value without a major impact to your net worth. It is all about ratios and what your net worth is versus what you're spending on a vehicle. Opinions vary on what your net worth should be before you buy a new vehicle, but I can safely say it should be well over $500,000 to make the math work for you. However, if you keep your vehicle for more than 15 or 20 years, then that is a whole different conversation.

Extended Warranties

If you want an extended warranty, *only* buy the manufacturer's extended warranty, as 3rd-party warranty companies may just close up shop and leave you with nothing except an empty wallet.

NUTSHELL

Car insurance is usually an afterthought, but you need to look at car insurance before you buy a car, not after. Shop around and get a minimum of three quotes for the same coverages. Not all insurance companies are created equal, and the lowest price is not always the best option. Look for insurance companies that are rated AM Best grade A or higher. Shop for car insurance at least every 2 years, especially if your rates go up and you haven't had an accident. Your vehicle is going down in value, so the cost to insure it should also decrease.

Buy an older vehicle at first (10–20 years old) and work up to a 3–5-year-old used vehicle, and always pay for it with cash. This will force you to buy only that which you can truly afford. Do not buy a new vehicle until your net worth is well over $500,000 in order to absorb the loss in value without a major impact on your net worth. Never lease, because you have all of the responsibility and obligations with none of the benefits that you would have when owning a vehicle outright. Do your research, test drive, and have a vehicle inspection before you buy.

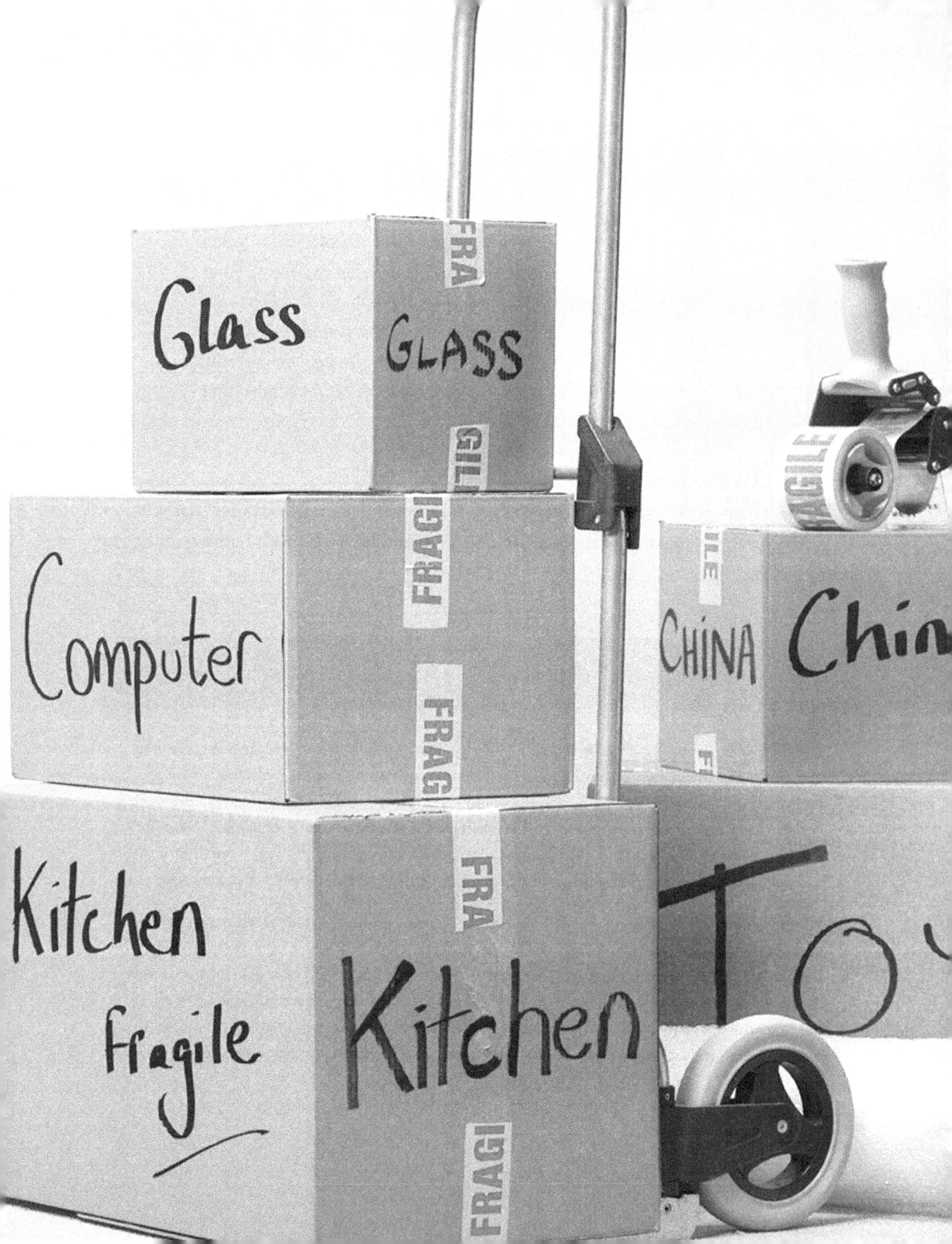

Glass
GLASS
FRA
GIL
Computer
FRAG
FRAG
CHINA
Chin
ILE
Kitchen
fragile
Kitchen
FRA
FRAGI
FRAGILE

A Temporary Situation
(Moving, Renters Insurance, and Renting Basics)

MOVING CAN BE BOTH exciting and daunting at the same time. It can also be a costly endeavor by itself, and you need to be aware of the moving scams that are out there. There are several that assist in moving your belongings, be it across town, across the state, across the country, or across the globe. If this is a just a temporary move (college or foreign exchange program of some type), this is relatively simple.

Moving on up or Just Moving

Temporary move

For a temporary move, you can just pack the essentials. Toothbrush, phone, wardrobe, shoes, socks, underwear—just the overall essentials. Don't worry if you're missing something. You can always pick it up once you get to your temporary housing. Normally you can make the move with the vehicle you already have at a very low cost, just buying some gas and some food.

Moving to an apartment locally

If you're moving locally, you can just make several trips to move all of your belongings from one place to another. Normally you can make the move with the vehicle you already have at a very low cost, but with a little more gas and a little more food.

Moving to an apartment over 100 miles away

Moving to an apartment over 100 miles away starts to get a little tricky and possibly more expensive. Making multiple trips is time-consuming and just a pain, so you really have *four options*.

Option 1: You can rent a moving truck and a car dolly, load up all your belongings including your car, make a one-way trip, and you're done. However, normally one-way trips are expensive because you are charged a drop fee for the moving truck.

Option 2: You can rent a moving truck, load up all your belongings but do a round trip, pick up your car, and make one final trip. This option is normally a less-expensive option because you are returning the moving truck to its original location, and no drop fee would be charged.

Option 3: You can have one of the storage companies drop off a storage unit in your parking lot. You load all your belongings into it, then call them to pick it up and deliver it to your new apartment, where you will unload your belongings. This option is normally a less-expensive option because you are not renting a moving truck.

Option 4: You pick out the must-have or must-keep items, sell the rest or donate what's left. You should be able to buy new and better belongings when you get to your new apartment. This option is normally the least-expensive option, and you get new belongings for your new apartment—only if it's in your budget, of course.

Dirk says . . .

YOU CAN ALWAYS MAKE MORE MONEY, BUT YOU CAN NEVER MAKE MORE TIME.

Moving from house to a house

Moving from one house to another house, whether locally or not is a big job and can take a lot of time and will cost you some money. This is where things can get really, really expensive if you're not careful. You can also get scammed by fly-by-night operations that call themselves "moving companies." Here you have *six options*:

Options 1–4 are the same as moving to an apartment over 100 miles away.

Option 5: You can hire a professional moving company that load, ship, store, and unload your belongings. Of course, this comes with a much higher cost than the move-it-yourself options.

Option 6: You can hire a professional moving company that can pack, box, load, ship, store, unload, and unpack your belongings. Of course, this also comes with a much higher cost than the move-it-yourself options.

With both options 5 and 6, you need to protect yourself from those by fly-by-night operations that call themselves "moving companies" and even some of the well-known players. How is this done? Well, it's back to doing some research. Check out the satisfactory rating reviews and their licenses at www.fmcsa.dot.gov. You also want to have a representative come out to your home so they can provide you with a *binding estimate.* If it's not a binding estimate, or if they don't offer a binding estimate, you need to call someone else. Legally, a mover can charge you whatever they want because it was only an estimate and not a binding estimate. In some cases, fly-by-night operations have refused to deliver the homeowner's belongings and held them for ransom until the homeowner paid up.

Also, you need to buy insurance to cover your items while in transit as they may become lost, stolen, or damaged. Check with your homeowners or renters insurance to see if moving insurance is included in your policy. If not, take advantage of the fact that the Federal Motor Carrier Safety Administration has mandated by federal law that moving companies offer at least two types of coverage:

1. **Full Value Protection**
    The mover is liable for the replacement value of damaged or lost items during the shipping.

2. **Released Value**
    This is the lowest-cost option of protection available for no additional charge. The protection is minimal, and liability is for no more than 60 cents per pound per article.

> If you select Released Value, you can buy separate liability insurance to cover the gap between the 60 cents per pound per article and the actual value of the article. Before purchasing insurance, check your homeowners or renters insurance policy to see if you're already covered.

Moving within a state?

Every state has regulations that govern movers. Make sure you check with your county or state's moving association before you hire that low-cost mover.

Moving to a different state?

All interstate movers that transport household goods across state lines must be registered with the Federal government. If they're not, don't take a chance, even if it's a good price.

Keeping Your Stuff Safe (Renters Insurance)

What is insurance?

The *Oxford Dictionary* defines *insurance* as: "An arrangement by which a company or the state undertakes to provide a guarantee of compensation for specified loss, damage, illness, or death in return for payment of a specified premium."

The Oxford dictionary defines *liabilities* as: "The state of being legally responsible for something. A thing for which someone is responsible, especially an amount of money owed.

In other words, you're transferring some of your financial risk to someone else by paying them a set amount of money at prearranged times."

What is renter's insurance?

Renters insurance is a liability policy that covers your personal property, items can be repaired or replaced in the event of theft; vandalism; riot or civil commotion; severe weather; fire; smoke; fire sprinklers; appliances; damage caused by vehicles or aircraft; explosions; falling objects; plumbing systems and issues related to damage from an HVAC system. It can also pay for expenses if the place you're living in becomes uninhabitable.

Items that are normally *not* covered are intentional destruction of property; neglect of property; damage from flooding; governmental seizure of property; nuclear hazard; or war.

Contacting multiple insurance companies to get a general idea of what your renter's insurance will cost you to live in a given area is the first step you should take before signing a rental agreement. You probably have a good idea of where you want to live. This gives you a starting point when shopping for renter's insurance. Now you can start asking targeted questions about the area such as what type of claims are most often filed within this area or neighborhood? How often are claims being filed within a given area? What is covered and not covered by your renter's insurance policy?

In most cases, renter's insurance is very inexpensive, because you're only insuring personal property such as clothes, electronics, tables, chairs, dishes, silverware and so on. Because you're not insuring the building or structure, the cost is very low in comparison to a homeowners policy.

Keep in mind, not all insurance companies or policies are created equal, and the lowest price is not always the best option. You will need to look at the ratings of the insurance company and what the overall experiences customers are having.

[one:un:uno]

Renting Basics

What is renting?

Renting is when you pay the owner of a dwelling a set amount of money every month to live in that dwelling. In most cases, this will be accompanied by a rental agreement or rental contract. In other words, you are paying money to someone else, but you will never own what you are paying for and by signing a rental agreement or rental contract you're stating that you will be following the rules stated within the agreement or contract. If you do not follow the stated rules outlined in the agreement or contract, you could be penalized and/or evicted from the dwelling.

Renting is not a bad thing despite what some people say. You may just be starting out, or maybe you just don't want to be tied down to a single location for a long period of time or you may not want the obligations that come with homeownership. These are all great reasons to rent. When you plan on renting a room, apartment, condo, or house, it's up to you to read and understand the contract. You need to know what you're responsible for and what the landlord is responsible for before signing your rights away. The landlord may say one thing and the contract says another . . . guess what? The contract will be enforced every time.

Why do landlords have you sign a contract? They want to protect their property in a legal manner, and they do this in writing with the rental agreement or rental contract. This way it's clear what obligation and rights each of you have under the rental agreement or rental contract.

There are federal laws that are in place such as anti-discrimination and habitability laws, you should know and understand these before you start looking for an apartment. You also need to research and understand your state's landlord and tenant laws; there may be laws in place that cover items such as security deposits and how much notice a landlord needs to give tenants if they want them to move out.

Security Deposits

This is normally equal to 1 month's rent, but it could be more depending on location and whether or not the location is furnished.

Before moving in, you need to protect yourself for when you plan to move out. Wait, what? You're planning ahead, document the condition of the property by taking photos and/or video of the property before you move in. This way when you're ready to move out, you're not being held responsible for something that was existing before you moved in!

During your stay, make sure you follow the rental agreement or rental contract. Some repairs may be your responsibility; don't assume it's the landlord's.

When you're ready to move on to bigger and better things, you need to make sure you're prepared to turn the property back over to the landlord in the same or better condition than when you moved in. A good cleaning from top to bottom, repairing any damage you may have caused, getting the carpets cleaned—maybe even patching and painting the walls if needed. Leave the property in better condition than when you moved in. Make sure you take photos and video of the property showing the condition before you move out. This can be done at the time of the walkthrough with the landlord. Having the "before move-in photos and video" and the "just before moving out photos and video" should almost guarantee the return of your full security deposit.

NUTSHELL

A do-it-yourself move will save you the most money. If you hire a professional moving company, you need to protect yourself by doing your research. Check out the satisfactory ratings, reviews, and the license of the moving company before choosing. You also want to get a binding estimate. Legally, movers can charge you whatever they want if they only provided you with an estimate and not a binding estimate.

Buy insurance to cover your items while in transit. Check with your homeowners or renters insurance to see if moving insurance is included in your policy. If not, get coverage through the moving company. The Federal Motor Carrier Safety Administration has mandated by federal law that moving companies offer at least two types of coverage: Full Value Protection and Released Value.

Renters insurance is a liability policy that covers your personal property. Renters insurance is very inexpensive, so there's no reason not to have it.

Renting is not a bad thing despite what some people say. It's up to you to read and understand the contract. You need to know what you're responsible for and what the landlord is responsible for before signing your rights away.

CHAPTER 15

College Knowledge

Warning!

THIS CHAPTER CAN CHANGE your life! I know, this is a bold statement, but it's a true statement nevertheless. Making choices about college needs to be a team effort. You being the parent or you being the child need to understand the nuts and bolts at a deeper level before moving forward with choosing a college.

Because these choices are so important, I'm taking you deeper and providing you with more technical information than in other chapters. This way you can really make the best decision for your wallet and your education.

How Can I Pay for College? I'm Not Rich!

Over **1.5 TRILLION DOLLARS** in student loan debt and rising! Yep, that's right—that's how much student loan debt is carried by Americans across the United States.

Are you one of those Americans who has student loan debt or is planning on taking out a loan for a higher education? What will this mean for you in the long term? How will it affect the rest of your life?

Taking out student loans *will* have a ripple effect on the rest of your life, as well as your financial life! The financial obligation you are taking on even before you have a job will have a huge impact on some of your most important life decisions such as having kids or being able to buy a house. It will most likely have an effect on your relationships with friends, family, and definitely with your significant other over time.

In addition to those issues, you will be emotionally affected by carrying around the constant reminder of that debt. Long-term and large amounts of debt will cause many emotions, including anxiety, stress, fear, anger, frustration, regret, denial, shame, embarrassment, resentment, and even depression.

Why? In most cases, figuring out how to pay for college comes after you choose the college you want to go to. By then, you are already way behind and you're putting your financial future at risk!

Most people are not thinking with the end in mind, let alone taking a step back to look at how to pay for college before picking a college. The typical thought process is, *Oh, well, my parents will help me pay for it,* or *I'll just take out a loan to pay for it.* Guess what? Your parents are most likely still paying off their own student loans, so they don't have the money to pay for your college, nor should they. You want to be an adult, so it's time to grow up and be an adult. You need to figure out how to pay for your education without relying on someone else to do it for you!

Start early when looking at ways to pay for college! The sooner the better. With college cost continuing to rise and outpace both the cost of inflation and medical insurance, planning ahead is key.

Dirk says . . .

HOW DO WE GROW AND GET BETTER?
BY DOING NEW THINGS.
THINGS THAT ARE HARD AT FIRST
GET EASIER OVER TIME.

Before paying the full cost of college, you may be able to test out of certain classes and receive college credits by doing so.

One option is the College Level Examination Program (CLEP), a test that costs about $100 versus $600 or so for a three-credit class at a community college and a lot more at university. Make sure the college you're going to attend will accept the CLEP credits; otherwise, you're just wasting your money. You can always check the College Board Searchable Database, but you will always need to confirm with the college just to make sure nothing has changed.

Another option is the Advanced Placement classes and exam (AP exam). These can help your application rank higher, and they can also show you where your academic interests and strengths lie. You also may receive college credits as well with this exam. However, some schools only use them to place you in a higher-level class but don't allow the credits to fulfill your credit requirements.

The following are ways to pay for college.

1. Scholarship
   - Both public and private scholarships are available.
   - A simple web search can show you all types of available scholarships. Some of the most common types of scholarships are merit based, student specific, career specific, need based, and location based.
   - The better your grades, the better chance you will have at meeting the sponsor's qualifications.
   - Scholarships come in all sizes and come from all types of sponsors. You do have to put some work into this process by applying for a scholarship,

but don't just apply for the large scholarships. The small and medium scholarships do add up and are most often overlooked—$500 is still $500 that you don't have to dip into your wallet for. Right?

- Start local. You have a better chance if you're applying for a scholarship from a local sponsor because they feel that they are helping out the community. It's good for the community, and it's good PR for the local sponsor. It's a win-win.

2. Grants

- Again, a simple web search can show you all types of available grants.
- Colleges, states, and the Federal government give out grants, which are sums that do not have to be repaid!
- The range can vary widely from a few hundred dollars to several thousand dollars depending on whether or not it's for a public or private school.

3. Military

- A big draw to any of the military branches is that you can receive training for free in a field that you qualify for. You could receive training to be a doctor, dentist, lawyer, pilot, engineer, and so on. Isn't that a great deal for a free education?

4. Employer Paid Education

- Some employers are looking for a specific set of skills and are willing to fund your education.
- Education reimbursement is very common. You will have to pay up front for the classes, but if you meet your employer's guidelines, they will reimburse you some or all of the cost of your classes.

5. Community College or Technical College

- States like Florida and Texas now offer 4-year degrees that cost around $12,000. That's all, for a 4-year degree! That is very affordable compared to $20,000+ a year for a traditional college. However, many community colleges still only offer 2-year degree programs.
- If 4-year degree programs are not offered at your community college or you don't want to go to a community college for all four years, just go for

the first two years. This will get your core classes out of the way and save you a lot of money at the same time.

- Technical colleges offer training for real-life skills that can be applied today in industries that need skilled team members. This is an option for those that are not interested in going to a traditional college.

6. **Pay-as-you-go option**
- Get a job and save your money so you can pay for the classes as you go.
- Work for the school. Normally they have some type of program that will reduce the cost of tuition. In some cases, your classes may be free.

7. **Living off campus**
- This can save you between $10,000 and $12,000 a year.

8. **Starting a 529 plan***
- This is a tax-advantaged investment account for education that is opened for a child, but anyone can be named the beneficiary: a friend, a relative, or even yourself. There are no income restrictions on either the beneficiary or the contributor who sets up a 529 plan.
- There are contribution limits, so reviewing and understanding the IRS tax code for a 529 plan is your best defense in avoiding any penalties or fees. You can also talk to your accountant or tax preparer for guidance. The tax code changes every year, so don't assume the 529 plan rules will stay the same from year to year.
- The Achieving a Better Life Experience (ABLE) account or 529A account may be an option for individuals with disabilities to pay for qualified disability expenses. Specific criteria must be met to be eligible for an ABLE account. If you do qualify, funds can be used as a supplement to government benefits that you may already be receiving. Annual contribution limits vary by state and can change from year to year, so you will need to verify the contribution limits each year. Contributions can be made by anyone, not just family members. Unfortunately the contributions are not tax-deductible.
- Earnings from the ABLE account will be not be taxed if used for a "qualified disability expenses." Qualifying expenses can change over time

so don't assume that because it qualified last year that it will qualify next year. The list below and many others may qualified as disability expense, but *you will need to confirm with your state, financial advisor, and tax preparer to be sure.*

>> Medical treatment
>> Special-needs transportation
>> Assistive technology
>> Housing
>> Education, tutoring and job training
>> Legal and administrative fees

- The Municipal Securities Rulemaking Board, or MSRB regulates both the 529 college savings plans and ABLE accounts, as they are both considered "municipal fund securities."
- The reason for the * is that unless your parents are out of debt and have disposable income, this option is off the table as far as your parents are concerned. However, relatives and grandparents may be in a better financial situation and could set up a 529 plan.

9. **Tax credit**
- This can change from year to year, but the IRS currently allows you to reduce your taxes after paying for tuition, fees, and books.

The last option . . .

10. **Taking out a loan**
- The *only* loan you should *ever* take out for higher education is a Federal loan, such as the Stafford loan. Federal loans have more flexible repayment options compared to private loans.
- Take the smallest amount possible! You will have to pay it back!

Options, options, and even more options. As you can see, there are multiple ways to pay for college without having to take out a loan.

Having the Knowledge to Pick the Right College

This is a huge decision that will change your life. You absolutely must pick the right college! You need to choose a college that is *right for you.*

Top 3 ways not to choose a college
1. You received an acceptance letter from a college.
2. Just because your friends are going there.
3. The college has a perceived status or prestige.

Top 5 things to avoid when choosing a college
1. Rushing to choose
2. Choosing a college on emotion
3. Following the crowd
4. Having to "be a legacy"
5. Going just to party

This is about you and no one else! Start early and take your time—make sure the college you want to go to will be a good fit for you!

Top 12 items to consider when choosing a college

1. Cost
2. Degree/Major availability
3. Campus size
4. Student life
5. Student body diversity
6. Current students' opinions of the college
7. What the college is really focused on
8. Student–Teacher ratio
9. Location
10. On-Campus housing options
11. Graduating data
12. School rankings

NUTSHELL

The best way to pay for your higher education is to have someone else pay for it! This can be done through scholarships, grants, joining the military, or even having your employer pay for it. If you have to pay out of pocket, pay-as-you-go is the next best way to pay for your higher education. If you take out a loan, you only want to take out a Federal loan, such as the Stafford loan, and avoid private loans altogether. Keeping your cost low is key. By living off campus and utilizing a community college or a technical school, you can substantially reduce the cost of your higher education to $15,000 or less for a 4-year degree. That's a financial win!

When choosing a college, start early and take your time. Make sure the college you want to go to will be a good fit for you. This is about you and no one else.

CHAPTER 16

Walking Down the Aisle

WEDDINGS CAN BE VERY expensive! Currently, a wedding can cost on average as much as a brand-new midsize SUV (depending on options). That's around $35,000! Yikes!

It's been a few years since Madalyn and I walked down the aisle. However I still have vivid memories of all the fun we had. I also recall all the decisions that we had to make to get there.

I know, trying not to worry about all of the details is extremely hard to do, but don't stress out, enjoy this time and don't worry if something goes wrong. Most people are not going to remember if anything went wrong, just that they had a great time on your special day.

If things get out of hand, the sky's the limit. You can get a 4-year degree for that and still have about $18,000 left over to invest (if you know where to go to college). You need to start with a budget first and foremost when planning your wedding. This will help you make decisions on what is truly a need versus a want. The wedding is about you and your soon-to-be spouse, not anyone else! Don't try to compete or compare your wedding to someone else's. You will be disappointed and just blow your budget. Are you getting the point? Be in agreement with your future spouse on what your needs and wants are for the wedding. (You will have many, many "discussions" about this topic, trust me.) Being creative will help you stay within your budget and help you and your future spouse work together to find solutions. This will be the first of many problem-solving challenges that you will face in your new life together. Why not start out as a team and work together?

Search the internet for creative ways to have an awesome wedding without breaking your piggy bank. This is your special day, and you may want to invite everyone you know, but that's just not practical. I'm sure you will do lots of research on your own and hear what experts say about what you absolutely need to make the wedding of your dreams come true. However, this is not a TV show or a movie where everything is perfect and money is no object. This is your life, and in most cases, money will be the biggest hurdle between your "dream wedding" and your actual wedding.

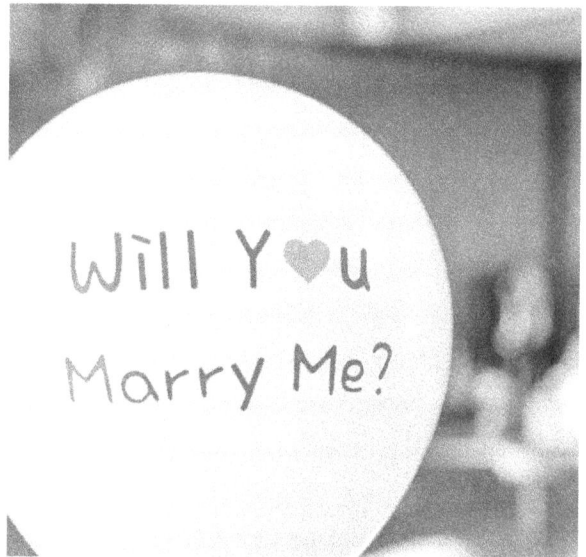

NUTSHELL

Weddings can be very expensive. Be in agreement on what your needs and wants are for the wedding. Search the internet for creative ways to have an awesome wedding without breaking your piggy bank. The wedding is about you and your soon-to-be spouse, not anyone else.

CHAPTER 17

To Will or Not to Will, That is the Question

HAVE YOU RECEIVED AN inheritance? If you have, the person you received the inheritance from probably had a will, and you were the one who benefited from someone else planning ahead. Do you really think not having a will is a good financial decision? Having the last word can be worth thousands, hundreds of thousands, or even millions of dollars to your loved ones. So, I will ask you again, do you really think not having a will is a good financial decision? A will can remind us of our own mortality, so most of us avoid talking about one, let alone actually sitting down and making one, but you have to remember this is not about you. It's about those who remain after you're gone! A will is a legal document that is enforceable by the law. A will is really for your family or loved ones. A will makes it so much easier on them and for them as they will be able to clearly understand your intentions and how you want your assets distributed.

The *Oxford Dictionary* defines will as "Expressing desire, consent, or willingness. Bequeath something to (someone) by the terms of one's will."

That means a will or testament is a document that instructs the executor, executrix (the person who handles your estate), or the government how you want your estate distributed and to whom you want it to be distributed. You may want to give portions of your estate to your family, friends, or to charity. Then again, maybe not, but this is your only chance to have your wishes carried out. Why not take it?

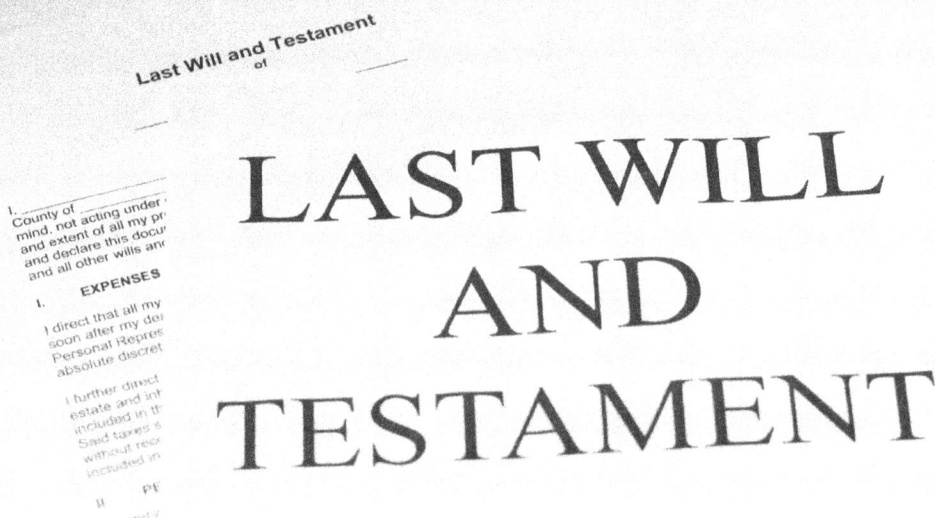

Here are a few reasons why you would want a will. Let's say you are a single parent with two kids *under* the age of 18. You and your best friend both agree that if anything should happen to either one of you, the other one would raise the other's kids. The unthinkable happens, and you die in an auto accident on the way to pick up your kids. Unfortunately, you do not have any living relatives, and without a will, your best friend would not be able to raise your kids. Your children would go right into foster care, where it is highly probable that they will be separated because most foster parents can only take one child in at a time. If you had a properly prepared will in the state that you lived in, documenting the agreement you had with your best friend, your wishes would be carried out as discussed.

Here's another scenario. What if you have property or money that you wanted to give to your friends or several charities instead of your family? If you do not have a will, it would normally go to your immediate family after going through a short probate process, but by having a properly prepared will in the state that you live in, you get to decide who will inherit your property, your money, and handle your estate.

If you have a complicated estate, such as a blended family, own a business, or don't feel comfortable using one of those DIY will makers online, have an attorney that specializes in wills, trusts, and estates draw up the will for you. You can save time and money by making a list of everything and identify who gets what. Be clear with your wishes, as this will make it easier for them to be carried out. You have the ability to set your family up for their future financially by using a will.

NUTSHELL

Making a great financial decision can last for years and years, even if you're not around. Taking care of your family should be your first priority. A will can help you do that, but most of us just don't get around to creating one. I don't see that as being acceptable; do you? So, why not make sure that your family is taken care of by having the last word in writing?

CHAPTER 18

Kids Are
Really Expensive!

FROM ALL THE RESEARCH I have done and from what I have heard experts say, kids are expensive! Plan on spending a lot of money if you are planning on having one. As with anything, depending on which part of the country you live in—heck, even which part of the city you live in—costs can vary tremendously.

WARNING

A little mind blowing is about to take place. You can expect to pay out of pocket somewhere around $250,000 for a single kid from birth to age eighteen! That is around $13,888.88 per year for a single kid! Wow! This typically includes food, clothing, insurance, childcare, transportation, and public education. This does not take into account any special circumstances, good or bad.

NUTSHELL

Kids are expensive! Be aware, be informed, and most of all be prepared. Having your financial house in order before having kids is the best way to insure you have more time to spend with your kids instead of working to make ends meet.

CHAPTER 19

My Home is
My Castle
(Insuring, Funding, and
Picking the Right Home for You)

Keeping Your Home and Stuff Safe (Homeowners Insurance)

Homeowners insurance is a policy that covers losses, damages, and assets within the home. It also provides liability coverage against accidents in the home or on the property. It can repair or replace items in the event of theft, vandalism, riot or civil commotion, severe weather, fire, smoke, fire sprinklers, appliances, damage caused by vehicles or aircraft, explosions, falling objects, plumbing systems, and issues related to damage from an HVAC system. It can also pay for expenses if the place you're living in becomes uninhabitable.

Items that are normally not covered are intentional destruction of property, neglect of property, damage from flooding, damage from earthquakes, governmental seizure of property, and nuclear hazard or war.

In other words, you are transferring some of your financial risk to someone else by paying them a set amount of money at prearranged times.

Contacting multiple insurance companies to get a general idea of what homeowners insurance will cost you to live in a given area is the first step you should take before settling on a specific house. You probably have a good idea of where you want to live already. This gives you a starting point when you're shopping insurance companies so you can ask targeted questions about the area, such as what type of claims are most often filed within the area or neighborhood. How often are claims being filed within a given area? What's covered and not covered within your homeowners insurance policy?

Homeowners insurance can vary greatly in cost due to a multitude of factors such as location, size of the house, the type of pets you may own, number of previous claims, amount of coverage, and most of all, the insurance company itself.

Keep in mind that not all insurance companies or policies are created equal, and the lowest price is not always the best option. You will need to look at the ratings of the insurance company and the overall experiences customers are having.

How can you keep your premiums low?

You can raise the deductible (out of pocket) from $500 to $750 or $1,000 or higher if you can afford it. The higher the deductible, the lower your premium. Make sure you have the money for your deductible set aside in the event you have to pay your deductible. Also, you can lower the coverage amounts to lower your premium, or you can do both to get an even lower premium.

Another way to keep your premiums low is *not* to file small claims with your insurance company. It is best to pay them out of pocket. Making claims will raise your premiums in the future. It may hurt your wallet at first, but at least you will not be hit with higher premiums for years and years to come.

> You may be able to save more if you bundle your car and homeowners with the same insurance company. This also applies to you car and rental insurance.

Bankrolling the Casa (Paying For Your House)

I can tell you that looking for your first house is exciting. Imagining all the possibilities and all the changes that you can make when it becomes yours can be endless. Man, that really is a lot of fun! How do you go from looking to owning? The default setting for us mere mortals is to run to a bank and take out a mortgage or two. Yes, I said "or two."

This will most likely be the biggest purchase you will ever make in your life! Think about it—the biggest purchase you will ever make in your life. Let that sink in for a few minutes, let that marinate . . .

This is a huge life event. It comes with responsibilities and obligations that you may breeze by when you're "looking for a house." But later you will realize those responsibilities and obligations that you overlooked, and it will be too late.

What are some of the obligations that will come with being a homeowner?

- Earnest money
- Down payment
- Closing costs
- Mortgage insurance
- Homeowners insurance
- HOA dues (homeowners' association)
- Property taxes
- Appliances
- Furnishings
- Maintenance, and so on

> Why do we use the saying, "I just bought a house"? The cold hard truth is you borrowed money from a bank to buy "your" house. The bank is allowing you to live there for two reasons—you are paying them an agreed-upon amount each month, and they are making a profit off of that arrangement. Just stop paying the bank and see what happens. You will find out right away who owns the house. The bank will kick your butt to the curb because they own it and you don't!

First-time home buyers

The best advice I can give you here is to try to be debt free before buying your first home! I, like most of you, heard from the people around me that you need to buy a house and stop wasting your money on rent. Let's do a little translation here. *You have people who are broke telling you how to be broke just like them.* Is that really a smart move?

Risk management is what it comes down to. Remember you are planning for the future by minimizing risk, and in life we have risks that we cannot control, but you can control what you do and which actions you take that will decrease those risks. Are you broke? By "broke," I mean you are making payments on everything, you have no emergency fund or savings, and you live paycheck to paycheck. If you're broke, adding the financial stress of a mortgage payment—plus home maintenance costs—would not be a smart move. I mention the home maintenance aspect, as it is normally overlooked until something breaks. These unexpected expenses in most cases will push you over the financial edge when you are broke. If you have lived through the dot com bubble, the housing bubble, The Great Recession, or the COVID-19 pandemic, you may have already experienced losing a job and know first hand the stress and worries that come with it, such as how you will put food on the table, keep a roof over your head, and pay your bills. As The Great Recession showed us, you could be out of work for months or even years. Keeping this in mind will help guide you when making your biggest financial decision.

> Think of your first home as a starter home, not your forever home! The fact is, your first home is not going to be your forever home. After a few years, your ideas of your forever home may change.
>
> The biggest factor is that your wallet will most likely not be able to support your idea of a forever home right away. You will need to work up to your forever home as this will lessen the stress on you and the stress on your wallet.

How to buy

The ideal way to buy a home is 100% cash. Yes, this takes more time, but you have no risk of losing your home because of not making a payment. If you are unable to pay for your new home with cash, at a minimum you need to have a down payment of 20%. Obviously, if you can put more down, you should. You also should not take out more than a 15-year mortgage. A down payment of 20% normally eliminates the need for PMI (private mortgage insurance), but this varies by lender.

Limit your spending on housing to a maximum of 25% of your take-home pay. By only spending 25% of your income on housing, you will have 75% of your income to save, pay other bills, and live life without the stress of a huge mortgage payment.

Option with a warning

Due to my own experiences of job losses in the past, the last time we took out a mortgage, we took out a 30-year mortgage but paid it as a 15-year mortgage. Then as time went on, we kept increasing the amount we paid until we were paying three times the minimum monthly payment. This allowed us to have a buffer in the event either of us had a job loss. However, if you do not have the discipline to take on this challenge, you may end up paying as agreed on a 30-year mortgage instead of paying it as a 15-year mortgage as you had planned.

Don't think you have to buy your dream home right away—in fact, you shouldn't. Don't compare what you are doing to what the broke people around you are doing or fall into the same trap of making payments because that's perceived as normal. You can always move up in house as you make and save more money.

In case you are not aware, I will state it here: PMI (private mortgage insurance) protects the mortgage company, not you.

Knowledge

You need to be armed with knowledge before thinking about getting preapproved and definitely *way* before looking for a house. Remember, the lender will always want to give you the maximum amount that you qualify for at the longest term possible. That way, they can make the most money off you. Just remember, the more you spend on housing, the less you will have for everything else. **You should never borrow the full loan amount you are preapproved for**. Instead, stay conservative and look for homes in a price range that will keep your mortgage payments within your budget and no more than 25% of your take-home pay.

Prequalifying for a mortgage

Prequalifying for a mortgage before you start looking for a house is the first step to making a good financial decision. By doing this, you get an idea of what kind of home you can afford and what the monthly payment will look like.

Most people only get one mortgage quote, but to get the best deal, you will need to get multiple quotes. Look to your local credit unions, small local banks, and online mortgage lenders. Credit unions can offer creative mortgages that can save you money, so check with them first.

When you're looking to prequalify for a mortgage, lenders will be pulling your credit in order to provide you a mortgage quote, this should also include the interest rate. This will typically lower your credit score slightly. To minimize this, you should get all your quotes within a 14-day period. By doing this, the numerous inquiries are instead treated as a single loan inquiry for a single property instead of multiple loan inquiries for multiple properties.

When applying for a mortgage, be aware you will see a variety of junk fees.

- Administrative fee
- Application fee
- Broker fee
- Courier fee
- Credit report fee
- Document preparation fee
- Origination fee
- Processing fee
- Wire transfer fee

These fees are just made up, so most of them can be negotiated down or removed altogether. You need to be your own advocate and challenge the lender on these junk fees. In reality, these fees are chump change to them, but most people don't challenge them, so they are able to make more money off the uninformed or the desperate.

Common Types of Home Loans

Conventional loan (fixed)

This is a loan normally issued by private lenders. These are not backed by any government agencies, and the lender is assuming all the risk.

Adjustable rate mortgage (ARM)

This is a loan with an interest rate that is variable (or floating) instead of a fixed interest rate like a conventional, FHA, or VA loan. The interest rate will change after the fixed term of the loan is over. For example, a 5/1 ARM is fixed for 5 years, and each year after that, the interest rate will either increase or decrease depending on which index the loan is tied to. This means that the monthly payments can go up or down after 5 years for the remaining duration of the loan.

Federal Housing Authority (FHA loan)

This is a mortgage that is insured by the Federal Housing Administration. Usually, FHA loans have a much lower down payment than other mortgages, normally 3.5% for credit scores of 580 and higher. First-time home buyers may be pushed toward this option to close the deal if they do not qualify for other types of loans. You will need to pay PMI or Private Mortgage Insurance, which protects the lender if you default on the loan.

Veteran's Administration (VA loan)

This one is self-explanatory. To qualify, you need to be a veteran or a surviving spouse of a veteran. You still need to meet additional requirements to qualify for a VA loan, such as service, credit, and income requirements. Private lenders such as banks, savings and loans, or mortgage companies offer guaranteed VA loans to eligible veterans for the purchase of a home. The guarantee replaces the protection the lender normally receives by requiring a down payment to obtain favorable financing terms. The guarantee means the lender is protected against loss if you fail to repay the loan. Guaranteed VA loans are normally more expensive than conventional loans. To cover the costs of the guarantee along with the costs involved when a VA loan goes into default, the VA charges an upfront fee to help pay for those costs.

Title insurance

When taking out a mortgage, you will have the option to purchase title insurance. It will be something you want to purchase. Title insurance protects both you and the lender(s). However, you will need to purchase *two policies*, an owner's policy that insures the new owner (you) and a lender's policy that insures the priority of the lender's security interest.

A title insurance policy insures against events that occurred in the past of the real estate property and the people who owned it.

15-year versus 30-year mortgage

Let's run some numbers to get a better understanding of what a 15-year and a 30-year mortgage looks like. I will use some typical numbers and factor a down payment for an income range between $60,000–$67,000. I will also include 25%–28% for taxes and insurance, which are typically included in a monthly mortgage payment. Taxes can vary widely, so I'm going to use $200 a month. Your monthly payments should range between $1,250–$1,400. Having a $25,000 down payment would mean you could afford a $161,000–$180,450 house on a 15-year, fixed-rate mortgage at 3.5% interest.

A 15-year mortgage breakdown

	Mortgage Amount	Interest Rate	Monthly Payment	Total Amount You Will Pay	Total Amount of Interest You Will Pay
15-year mortgage	$ 161,000.00	3.5%	$ 1,150.96	$ 207,173.04	$ 46,173.04

A 30-year mortgage breakdown

	Mortgage Amount	Interest Rate	Monthly Payment	Total Amount You Will Pay	Total Amount of Interest You Will Pay
30-year mortgage	$ 161,000.00	3.5%	$ 722.96	$ 260,266.70	$ 99,266.75

By paying the agreed amount of $722.96 per month over your 30-year mortgage, you end up paying $53,093.71 more for the same house! What could you do with an additional $53,093.71?

Existing homeowners

Refinance to a lower mortgage rate and a shorter term! Most of us get busy with life and overlook some of the easy ways to save money. This can be a *two-for-one*. You can lower your interest rate and shorten the term of your mortgage. You may have not looked at rates in a while. This could save you hundreds of dollars each month and tens of thousands over the life of your mortgage. Check with your existing mortgage company first to see if they will refinance without fees or an appraisal. Check online for the best rates.

> A reverse mortgage or home equity conversion should be an absolute last resort if you are house-rich and cash-poor. It is pitched as a great solution, but like anything else, the lenders need to get paid, and they normally do it with high fees and low offers. Before you sign on the line, get some advice.

Dirk says . . .

YOUR HAPPINESS IS *NOT* DEFINED BY OTHER PEOPLE'S EXPECTATIONS, ESPECIALLY YOUR FAMILY'S.

Closing costs

I'm sure you have heard the term "closing costs." This refers to the costs over and above the purchase price of the house. This includes home inspection, lender fees, appraisal fees, attorney fees, title insurance for the lender, owner's title insurance for you (most people do not protect themselves; they protect the lender), escrow fees, and interest. Let's run some quick numbers to show you what this means. Suppose your budget is $210,000. In order to stay at or below your budget number, you would need to purchase a home for $200,000 or less as closing costs can run 2%–5% of the purchase price of the home. That 2%–5% converts into real money that you will need to bring to the closing table. That translates to $4,000–$10,000 in additional money that you will be required to fork over. That's a chunk of change that has to come from somewhere or you are not closing the deal on that house.

> This brings up a great point. If everyone is talking in percentages, *stop!* What I mean is if the attorney, lender, or the real estate agent is *not* telling you how much (as in dollars) it is going to cost you, just stop them until they give you an actual dollar amount. As you can see above, 2%–5% does not sound like much, but it can add up quickly.
>
> By law, the lender must provide you with a good-faith estimate of the closing costs three days before the closing. This sets expectations before arriving at the closing table and also allows you time to review the documents and find any issues, such as a misspelled name or incorrect address, thus avoiding any delays to the closing.

A Few Things You Need to Do Before Closing

1. Conduct a final walkthrough of the property at least the day before.
2. Confirm items have been addressed that were part of the contingency process. If they have not, stop the process until the items are addressed, or withdraw your offer.
3. You may want your own real estate attorney at the closing (as the closing attorney is representing the lender's interest, not yours).
4. Unless the items that were promised to be addressed are listed in the contract, the seller has no obligation to do anything that was promised after closing (this is known as a survival clause).
5. Bring some extra cash with you to the closing, as the closing costs may be slightly off, and the closing attorney will typically not accept a personal check. If you do not have the funds with you, it will delay the closing.

> If you have no debt, you may not have a credit or FICO score and may need to search for a mortgage company that underwrites its own mortgages.

I Want a Big House and I Cannot Lie (How to Choose a House)

Choosing a house can be so much fun as well as daunting, especially if it is your first house. This is going to sound cold, but your best bet is to remove as much of your emotions from this process as possible. Your emotions will make you spend well past your budget, and you *will* regret it every time you have to make a mortgage payment instead of doing something fun. That is, unless your idea of fun is making mortgage payments.

I know, I know, you want a nice house with a nice big yard, and you are going to fall in love with the right house as soon as you see it, and it's just going to feel right. And who do I think I am, telling you to take your emotions out of buying a house, because everything is just going to work out perfectly, so I should stop being a dream crusher! Right?

Wrong! Most of us plan based on how things are going or how things have gone in the recent past, thinking nothing but good things will happen in our future. That is not exactly how things work out, as those of us that have been around *four or five decades* and have been able to look at our own past as well as world history can tell you with absolute certainty. Life will throw you for a loop or two, whether you want it to or not. This is one guarantee I can make no matter who you are: life happens!

Dirk says . . .
TRADE SHORT-TERM PAIN FOR LONG-TERM GAIN.

A house is most likely the single largest purchase that you will make in your life. You will want to have a clear head, focusing on the facts, not your feelings, when you are ready to sign those papers. If you base the purchase of your house on facts that fall within a framework, criteria, and budget you planned out well in advance of looking for a house, you will be much happier in the long term. Is that not the end goal, to be happy with the house you picked?

What is the framework and/or criteria that I need to choose the right house for me or the right house for me right now? It's a checklist. That is the main ingredient in the magic formula—a checklist. First, you need to start with a budget number in stone that cannot increase no matter what. I am not talking about the one the lender is telling you that you are approved for, either!

The budget number is the most important part of the checklist, period, end of story! Got it? Everything after that is easy and just a matter of checkmarks. Take a look at the "How to Choose a House Checklist."

How to Choose a House Checklist

Budget: $_____

LOCATION

	Need	Want	N/A		Need	Want	N/A
Urban Location				Rural Location			

SPECIFIC LOCATION

Quiet or Secluded				Walking or Golf Cart Community			
Lake/Ocean View				Cul-de-Sac			
Mountain View				The Heart of the City			
City Skyline View				Nice Suburban Neighborhood			

ITEMS TO CONSIDER BASED ON LOCATION

Min. Distance to Work ____				New Neighborhood			
Max. Commute Time to Work ____				Established Neighborhood			
Emergency Service Response Times				Gated Community			
Cell Service Reliability				Limited Building Access (Security)			
Utility Reliability (Power, Water, Gas, Sewer)				Access to Top-Ranked Public Schools			
Min. Distance to Grocery and Retail Stores ____				Access to Top-Ranked Private Schools			
Access to Public Transportation				Parks, Green Space, or Dog Parks			

HOUSE SPECIFICS

Min. Age of the Home ____				Crawl Space (Open)			
Max. Age of the Home ____				Crawl Space (Sealed)			
Min. Sq. Footage of the Home ____				Basement			
# of Story Home ____				Private Garage			
Min. Age of the Roof ____				Min. # Car Garage ____			
Attic Space Built for Storage				Parking Structure			
Max. Age of the HVAC System ____				Street Parking			
Max. Age of the Water Heater ____							

HEATING AND A/C (Common Heating Options: Electric / Natural Gas / Propane / Solar / Wood / Fuel Oil / Steam)

Energy Efficient				Heat Pump			
Central Heating and Air				Boiler			
Fireplace				Electric Baseboard Heater			
Wood Stove/Pellet Stove							

EXTERIOR

Low Maintenance Exterior				Deck			
Large Yard (Fenced-In)				Patio			
Large Yard				Pool			
Small or No Yard				Sunroom			
Porch				Outside Storage/Buildings			
Breezeway				Gardens/Landscaping			

INTERIOR

Open Concept				Efficient Kitchen Layout			
Master Bedroom				Ample Kitchen Storage			
Master Bedroom with Walk-in Closet				Ample Kitchen Work Surface			
Master Bathroom				Laundry Room			
Min. # of Bedrooms _____				Ampule Laundry Room Storage			
Bedroom Closet Space				Hardwood Floors			
Min. # of Bathrooms _____				Granite Countertops			
Ample Bathroom Storage Space				Finished Basement			
Min. # of Inside Storage Closets _____				Handicap Accessible			
Pantry				Mud Room			

NOTES

Head over to DirkWrites.com and sign up for the Inside Scoop!
Receive a FREE copy of the How to Choose a House Checklist and a BONUS
resource. Only those who sign up will find out what the BONUS is
and how it can help you make better financial decision.

Actually looking for a house

Now that you have completed your "How to Choose a House Checklist," you can move on to actually looking for a house that fits your budget, framework, and/or criteria. There is no better place than the internet to start looking for a house! You can just type in your budget as well as your other criteria and bam, you are able to see hundreds and hundreds of houses without even leaving your living room! Doing this will help you get in tune with pricing, styles of houses, types of neighborhoods, types of communities, and the list goes on and on. Then you can start fine tuning your "How to Choose a House Checklist," ultimately narrowing the list down to an area that fits your budget, framework, and/or criteria.

Now you can start physically looking at houses in the area you are interested in. It may look great online, but in person you may not get that same warm fuzzy feeling as when you were in your PJs on the couch. At some point, you will most likely want to work with a real estate agent to help you pinpoint the house that will be your home. It can also be a challenge to find the right real estate agent who will get you into the right home for you, not for them ($$$).

Choosing the right real estate agent

Just like choosing the right house, you need to choose the right real estate agent for you. You need a great real estate agent who has at least 10 years of experience as a full-time agent, has sold at least 200 homes (this number may be lower in rural areas), and knows the market as well as the area you're interested in. Most importantly, you want an agent who will respect your budget while working with your best interest in mind and is on your side (a buyer's agent).

> If all the boxes are checked above, but you are feeling pressured by the agent, pull the plug. They are being paid on commission. As the price of the houses you are looking at goes up, so does their commission. A phrase you may hear is, "I have a listing that is just outside your price range, but it has almost everything you are looking for . . . Would you like to take a look at it?" Stop and ask them if you were not clear on the budget you have to work with. They do not have to pay the mortgage. You do! Stick to your budget.

You need to do your research, go old school, drive the area you're interested in, and look at the listing agents' signs in the yards. You will see a trend after a while, and usually two or three agents will keep popping up. Stop in at an open house and talk to them see them in action. No better way to see how they will treat you than when someone else is paying them to sell their house.

Here are a few questions you need to ask them.

1. Is this their full-time job?
2. How many years have they been a real estate agent?
3. Which area of town do they specialize in?
4. How many properties have they sold in the last month, in the last six months, and in the last year?
5. Why should I pick you as my real estate agent?
6. Ask for references.
7. Make sure your personalities do not clash (no-brainer on this one, but it happens).

NUTSHELL

Homeowners insurance is a policy that covers losses and damages as well as assets within the home. It also provides liability coverage against accidents in the home or on the property. Homeowners insurance can vary greatly in cost due to a multitude of factors such as location, size of house, type of pets, number of previous claims, amount of coverage, and the insurance company itself.

A 15-year, fixed-rate mortgage is the longest mortgage you should take out; otherwise, you cannot afford the house you want to purchase. If you take out a mortgage, keep it simple. Do not take out an atypical mortgage to get that house, because in the end, it will most likely cause you a headache.

When you are in the process of choosing a house, do not exceed your budget, and do not let your emotions make the choice for you. You do not want to end up regretting it every month when you make your mortgage payment, do you? Use the How to Choose a House Checklist to help you narrow down your needs and wants. Look at lots and lots of houses online to help dial in your needs to a specific area. Look for a qualified full-time real estate agent that has ten years of experience, has sold at least 200 houses, and specializes in the area you are interested in.

CHAPTER 20

Taking Care of Business

(Other Types of Insurance You Need or Need to Know About)

THIS WILL HELP YOU get a better understanding of some of the most common types of insurance that are available and why it may be something you need but just don't know it.

What is Insurance?

The *Oxford Dictionary* defines insurance as "An arrangement by which a company or the state undertakes to provide a guarantee of compensation for specified loss, damage, illness, or death in return for payment of a specified premium." This is the same definition I have used thoughout the book when referencing "What is insurance?"

In simple terms, you are transferring risk and/or financial burden to an insurance company or the state because you have entered into a contract and are paying them to take on some of the risk and or financial burden.

Most of us don't even think about insurance except when we are starting a new job (all the paperwork), when it's time to renew an existing policy, and when we need it or when we wished we had it. It's not a fun or sexy topic to talk about, and it's probably not even in your Top 20 things to talk about *this year*. However, you will need to move it up the chain of your priorities as you come to understand why insurance is such an important part of your financial success.

> *Never invest* through an insurance company! Insurance companies specialize in insurance, not investing. They charge high fees, and the returns are small even if they are guaranteed. You're not going to buy an insurance policy from an investment company, are you? So why would you invest with an insurance company?

Disclaimer

I am not a licensed insurance agent, nor do I claim to know how you should choose the life insurance policy that best suits your needs. You are responsible for your own research and choice of policy.

Let's start out with taking a look at life insurance.

What is Life Insurance?

It's insurance that pays out a sum of money either on the death of the insured person or after a set period. I'm sure you're asking, "Why do I need life insurance? What good is it going to do me if I'm dead?" I've asked the same questions myself. Well, sorry to tell you this, but life insurance is not about you or for you! It's about your family and what they will need in order to maintain the same income each month they had before you died. It is simply income replacement. However, in some cases, you may not need life insurance because that income will not need to be replaced.

Right out of the gate, the confusion is under way. Why is it called "life insurance" instead of "death insurance"? In most cases, the benefit is paid out *when* someone *dies*, not when someone lives. It comes down to marketing; it is all about the marketing! Would you really want to talk about your own death or buy something called "death insurance"? Well, would you?

Insurance can be very confusing, especially when the names that are being used are almost identical! It seems like the insurance industry is creating "new" products or rebranding old products all the time just to keep the confusion in play. Be informed and understand what you are buying and what it does and does not do for you. I cannot stress enough how important it is to understand what you are buying, not what you are being sold.

Take a look at some of the names being used for life insurance and why just the names alone can be confusing.

Common Types of Life Insurance

These are some of the common types of life insurance:

- Term life insurance
- Whole life insurance
- Universal life insurance
- Guaranteed universal life insurance
- Indexed universal life insurance
- Variable universal life insurance
- Variable life insurance
- Permanent life insurance
- Equity indexed life insurance
- Guaranteed issue life insurance
- Simplified issue life insurance
- Accidental death and dismemberment insurance
- And many, many more that I have not listed

Wow, is your head spinning yet? Well, mine is, and I wrote the darn chapter! You can see why insurance is not a fun or sexy topic to talk about, yet it can be very important to you and your family.

These are the three most common types of life insurance policies: term life insurance, whole life insurance, and universal life insurance. The two most *heavily pushed* life insurance policies are whole life and universal life insurance. They are pushed hard because the sales agent gets a *huge commission* on the sale. That is a big win for them but may not necessarily be the best choice for you.

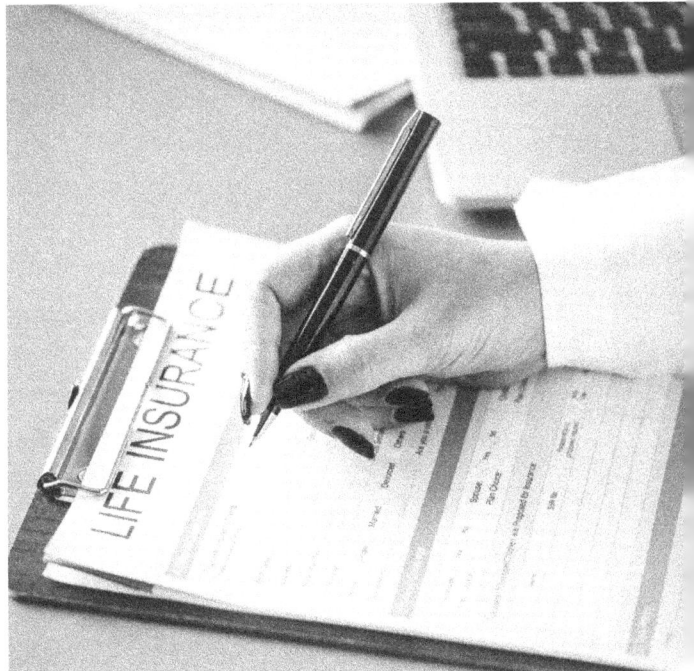

1. Premiums on life insurance policies can typically be paid monthly, quarterly, semiannually, or annually. Typically, the more times you pay, the more times you will be paying an added service fee.

2. You may or may not need a medical examination that would include a verbal medical history review to qualify for life insurance by some insurance companies.

Term Life Insurance

Term life is simply life insurance that covers you for a specific amount of time—typically 5, 10, 20 or 30 years. Upon your death, it pays out to the beneficiary that you have selected. Normally policies that do not require medical examinations have higher premiums.

In most cases, for us mere mortals, this is the *only* type of *life insurance* policy you need. It is simple to understand and wallet friendly. What more could you ask for?

There are only *three main questions* you will need to answer, although other factors may be involved, prompting you to ask additional questions. Answer them in the following order to find your specific answer.

1. **Do I really need term life insurance?**
   - Are you married?
   - Do you have children?
   - Does anyone depend on you financially?
   - Do you have a mortgage?

2. **How long do I need to have term insurance?**
   - How old are your children?
   - When will your mortgage be paid off?

3. How much term insurance do I need?
   - To keep it simple, you should buy 6–10 times your annual income. Coverage typically starts at $100,000 and goes up. For example, if you make $50,000 a year, you should buy a term life insurance policy somewhere between $300,000 and $500,000.

Single

If you do not have kids and no one is dependent on you financially, there is not much of a reason to buy life insurance. This is because your income will not need to be replaced as you are the only one dependent on your income.

Single with kids, or married with or without kids

If you are not single or you have dependents, then all the other answer combinations point toward you needing life insurance for the longest duration as possible. Your income will need to be replaced if you die, and life insurance can do this for those that depend on your income to live comfortably.

Whole Life Insurance

This is a policy that covers you for your whole life and has a built-in savings component. As with term insurance, upon your death, it also pays out to the beneficiary you have selected. Normally, policies that do not require a medical examination have higher premiums. For those who make above $400,000, this may be something to look into for some of the reasons listed below. For the rest of us, term would most likely be the best route.

Whole life insurance has a few more wrinkles just to make it a little more complicated.

1. First, the premium (your payment) is much higher than the premium for term life insurance.

2. It offers a cash value accumulation or a savings component. Part of your premium is directed here each time you pay your premium, although it will take from *12–15 years* to accumulate any meaningful cash value.
   - Cash value returns are typically guaranteed, but the returns are much, much lower than if you invest outside of the insurance policy. Meaning, you will not do as well or as poorly if you would have invested that same amount directly into the stock market with a low-cost investment broker.

- A portion of the cash value can be borrowed (a loan that will need to be paid back) during the policy.
- Additional fees may be associated with using the cash value option as each policy and provider is unique.

3. **It may be used as an estate-planning tool in some cases.**
   - The cash value builds tax deferred until it is withdrawn. This may or may not create a tax burden that will need to be paid.
   - Consult your tax advisor when it comes to tax-related items before you act. This will save you money and headaches.
   - If you have a high net worth, this is an option you may want to look at.

Dirk says . . .

DO NOT MIX INVESTING AND INSURANCE. KEEP IT SIMPLE; KEEP THEM SEPARATE.

Universal Life Insurance

This is a policy that covers you for your whole life and has a savings component as well as flexibility when it comes to the premiums. As with term and whole life insurance, upon your death, it also pays out to the beneficiary you have selected. Normally, these policies do not require a medical examination and have higher premiums.

Universal life insurance is like whole life but with even more wrinkles.

1. **First, the premium (your payment) is much higher than term life insurance but lower than whole life insurance.**
   - The premiums and the amount of insurance can be decided by you but are subject to policy minimums.
   - You must make every payment on time, or you risk losing the guarantee and forfeiting the policy.

2. **It offers a cash value accumulation or a savings component. Part of your premium is directed here each time you pay your premium, although it will take from *12–15 years* to accumulate any meaningful cash value. This can typically be linked to investments.**

- Cash value returns are guaranteed, but the returns are much lower than if you invest outside of the insurance policy.
- A portion of the cash value can be borrowed (a loan that will need to be paid back) during the policy.
- Additional fees may be associated when using the cash value option as each policy and provider is unique.

3. **It may be used as an estate-planning tool in some cases.**
   - The cash value builds tax deferred until it is withdrawn. This may or may not create a tax burden that will need to be paid.
   - Consult your tax advisor when it comes to tax-related items before acting, to save you money and headaches.

4. **The death benefit may be flexible.**
   - The death benefit can be paid out on its face value.
   - A $100,000 policy would pay out $100,000 as the benefit less any fees or loans that may have not been paid back previously.

The death benefit varies with your policy account value. This would be the face value plus the cash value amount of the policy. For example, a $100,000 policy with $5,000 cash value would pay out $105,000 as the benefit less any fees or loans that may have not been paid back previously.

Disability Insurance

You have a 60%–80% chance of being disabled at some point during your working career, depending on which experts you're listening to.

Disability insurance comes in two forms, short-term disability (STD) and long-term disability (LTD). In most cases, STD and LTD are offered by your employer as options. You do not have to buy them, but most of the time it will be a cost savings to you due to the group buying power of the company thus lowering your cost. If you are self-employed, you will need to look at an individual policy.

Short-Term Disability

Short-Term disability (STD) is coverage that can last for a few weeks up to 2 years depending on the policy that was issued. This also depends on whether it's a group policy or an individual policy. As the name implies, it's "short term" (Ha, no confusion on this one).

- The waiting period before your short-term disability insurance would pay out varies by insurer and by the policy issued but is typically 0–14 days and then you will start to receive your weekly check.
- Short-term disability typically replaces only 60% to 70% of your base salary.

Long-Term Disability

Long-Term disability (LTD) is coverage that normally starts after your short-term disability has ended. Long-Term disability can last until your disability ends or until the benefit ends after a certain period of time or at retirement age, depending on the policy that was issued. This also depends if it's a group policy or an individual policy. As the name implies it's "long term" (Ha, no confusion on this one either).

- The waiting period before your long-term disability insurance pays out varies by insurer and by the policy issued, but typically 90 days after your disability begins, you will start to receive your monthly check.
- Long-Term disability typically replaces only 40% to 60% of your base salary.

That was the simple part of explaining short-term disability (STD) and long-term disability (LTD). Now we get into some of the protections and options associated with those policies. We are only going to go over the two that are most common, then just list out the other options that are available.

Non-cancelable

- As long as you pay the premiums, the insurance company cannot cancel the policy and must give you the right to renew each year without a premium increase.

Guaranteed renewable

- This allows you to renew the same policy with the same coverage and cannot be canceled by the insurance company. The insurance company has the ability to raise your premiums and will most likely do so over time, but they cannot single you out. They must raise the premiums on all policyholders who have the same rating class.

Other types of disability insurance policies are available.

1. Additional insurance purchase options
2. Coordination of benefits
3. Cost-of-living adjustment
4. Residual or partial disability rider
5. Return of premium
6. Waiver of premium provision
7. Business overhead expense disability insurance
8. Own occupation disability insurance (those with specialized training such as a doctor, lawyer, dentist)

Umbrella Insurance

Umbrella insurance is extra liability insurance that would be used after your home or auto policies have been exhausted. It also may provide coverage for claims that may be excluded by other liability policies including slander, libel, false arrest, and liability coverage on rental units you own. It also covers damage to property, injuries, some personal liability situations, and certain lawsuits.

Ordinarily, if you are debt free and have accumulated assets and wealth, it is an added layer of protection that helps you keep what you have worked so hard to achieve. The cost for a $1,000,000 umbrella policy is a few hundred dollars a year, and for each million after that, the cost only goes up slightly.

Long-Term Care Insurance

Long-Term care insurance is a policy that assists you outside of your medical coverage. It helps cover daily needs over extended periods of time. This includes disabilities, chronic illnesses, or other conditions where you would need help with bathing, dressing, and eating, which can be provided by professionals, therapists, or nurses.

This type of insurance is not cheap, and the premiums increase over time and could break your bank account.

There are several types of long-term care insurance policies.

1. Individual plan
2. Employer-Sponsored plans
3. Plans offered by organizations
4. State partnership programs
5. Joint policies

Typical services that may be covered include:

1. Nursing home
2. Assisted living
3. Adult day care services
4. Home care
5. Home modifications
6. Care coordination
7. Future service options

This type of insurance is in a state of flux, and changes happen on a regular basis. As you get older and into your mid to late 50s, you should look into getting some type of long-term care insurance.

Longevity Insurance

Longevity insurance is a policy that guarantees you a lifetime of income and typically starts paying you between the ages of 80–85. However, your monthly payout will be determined by how much you originally deposited, when you made the deposit, and when you start to receive distributions. Not a bad deal for you after age 80, especially because no one knows how long we are going to live. Knowing you're not going to run out of money can give you and your family peace of mind.

> Cancer insurance, accident insurance, and mortgage life insurance are all considered single-purpose insurance policies. These policies are in most cases a ripoff because they only cover a single issue.

NUTSHELL

Life insurance is about income *replacement* so your family does not have to worry about how they are going to make ends meet without your income. Keep it simple and save money by choosing a term life insurance policy. If you have no one financially dependent on you, you really do not need life insurance. Short-Term disability (STD) and long-term disability (LTD) insurance are a *must*, as you have a 60%–80% chance of being disabled at some point during your working career.

Umbrella insurance is extra liability insurance that could be used after your home or auto policies have been exhausted. It's an added layer of protection that helps you keep more of what you have attained.

Long-Term care insurance is a policy that assists you outside of your medical coverage by covering daily needs. This type of insurance is not cheap. Start looking at this once you're nearing your mid to late 50s.

CHAPTER 21

Start with
The End in Mind!
(Planning for Retirement
and Investing)

OKAY, HERE IS WHERE I get into some heavy and detailed information. This chapter can help set you up for a comfortable life so you can decide to stop working because you want to stop working not because you have to.

This is important!

It's easier and cheaper than ever to start saving for retirement, and the sooner you start, the sooner you can retire comfortably. How would you like to retire in your mid to late 40s, leaving you years and years to enjoy life, being able to do what you want, when you want? The opportunities are endless when you have that kind of financial freedom.

That sounds pretty awesome! Right?

This is where all the doubts and disbelief start creeping in followed by statements, reasons, excuses about why it's not possible.

1. Nobody can do that.
2. I plan on working until I die anyway, so I don't need to save for retirement.
3. I can save for retirement later.
4. I'm a single parent.
5. I have to pay for my kid's college.
6. I don't make enough money to save for retirement. I'm barely getting by now.
7. Someone is going to rip me off if I invest with them.
8. I don't trust "investment people" because they just want to take all my money.
9. I don't understand anything about investing, so I'm better off not investing.
10. I'm so far in debt that I can't afford to save for retirement.

Do you want a better life? Do you want to be able to do what you want to do, when you want to do it? If you do, it's going to take work, planning, and most of all taking action—the "doing" part of it. This will also take dedication and determination to achieve early retirement. The sad fact is that most people do not start thinking about retirement until they are close to or in their 40s. Kind of hard to retire in your 40s if you don't start thinking about it until you're in your 40s, right?

Starting with the end in mind gives you a point or place to focus on. Then you can start to figure out what you need to do to get there. Without a specific point or place in mind, you have an extremely low chance of reaching your target. Minor financial adjustments at the beginning of your working life will greatly benefit you when you're ready to retire. While others will need to work to make ends meet, you'll be on the beach, the golf course, or traveling. Doesn't that sound like a great idea?

When you're young, the word "retirement" is such a foreign idea that you are most likely to dismiss it without a second thought. But as you get older and closer to that golden age or the promised land of retirement, you start to realize how important retirement planning is. Unfortunately, we don't have time machines (yet) so we are unable to change our past. The good news is it's never too late to start saving for your future, so start *today*.

Planning for retirement even before you graduate high school would be best. At such a young age, time is your friend. You would have decades to save and invest, and your money will be making money for far longer than almost anyone you will ever know that it's not even funny. This will dramatically change the course of your life and would put you *20–25 years ahead* of when most people *start thinking* about planning for retirement. Just think how much different your life could be! Really, how different would your life be?

I know this is a difficult concept to grasp, and for most of you, this period in your life has passed, but you can still spread the word to your kids and grandkids, friends, and neighbors, starting them out on the right path and giving them a chance at a better life than what you had. That's what it's all about—giving your kids a better life than you had.

We'll run the numbers to see why it's so important to start saving early. Mark and Ted's lives will be dramatically different just by choosing when they start saving for retirement. Say Mark and Ted have similar incomes, and both are twenty-five at this time.

Mark's parents have always shared with Mark how important saving for retirement is. By saving for retirement as soon as he could, the odds are in his favor. He will be able to retire early and truly enjoy retirement. They also explained that it's his responsibility to save and not rely on Social Security or government handouts to make ends meet in his golden years. They explained that the advantage of saving earlier is *time*, having more time for your money to build on itself because compounding interest is the key to building wealth.

Mark starts saving for retirement at age 25 by funding a Roth IRA and saving the maximum amount of $6,000 per year. Using an 8% average annual rate of return, **Mark will have $1,554,339 accumulated in his Roth IRA by the time he reaches age 65.**

Ted's parents never talked to him about saving for retirement, as *they do not talk about money in their family.* However, his parents have always struggled to make ends meet, leaving Ted with the impression that this is normal and how life is lived. Ted's not thinking about retirement at this time. He wants to live life and have some fun! What's the hurry, anyway? He's got the next 40 years to save for retirement. Right?

Ted is having fun and living life, but the next thing he knows, 15 years have gone by. He's now 40 but has not saved any money for retirement. This becomes a wakeup call for Ted, and he begins funding a Roth IRA, thinking he can make up for lost time and it's not too big of a deal because he will just start saving the maximum amount of $6,000 per year, so he should be okay. Ted is sadly mistaken. Using the same 8% average annual rate of return as Mark had, **Ted will *only have* $438,636 accumulated in his Roth IRA by the time he reaches age 65.**

$1,554,339 VERSUS 438,636. That is a *huge* difference!

Mark will have over one million more dollars than Ted just by starting 15 years earlier.

Dirk says . . .
TIME IS THE ULTIMATE EQUALIZER.

Important side note

Before we go any further, I need to make very clear the difference between saving and investing.

Saving = Safe

- In economics, savings is the amount that is left after spending. In banking, savings refers to savings accounts, which are short-term, interest-bearing deposits with a bank or other financial institution.
- Putting money into a savings or a money market account with a bank or credit union that is insured by either the FDIC (Federal Deposit Insurance Corporation) for banks or by the NCUA (The National Credit Union Administration) for credit unions means you have no risk of losing your money as long as you are under insurable limits. Currently this is $250,000 per depositor, per insured bank, for each account ownership category.
- Savings or a money market accounts are good for parking your money in the short term. This includes saving for vacations, taxes, and birthday or holiday gifts.

- Savings or money market accounts are not good for making money. You will make a very small amount of interest, and I mean a very small amount of interest on your money.
- Bottom line is no risk, no reward. Savings and money market accounts are safe.

Investing = Opportunity and Risk

- Investing is the strategic purchase or sale of assets in order to produce income or capital gains.
- When investing, you are looking for an opportunity to have your money make money. This is the reason most people invest.
- When you are investing, you are taking a risk! The risk is that you can lose some, most, or all of the money you invested. Unlike savings or money market accounts, your money is *not* insured by the FDIC or NCUA.
- What you choose to invest in will determine the amount of risk you put your money at. The most commonly referred to levels of risk are conservative, moderately conservative, moderately aggressive, aggressive, and very aggressive.

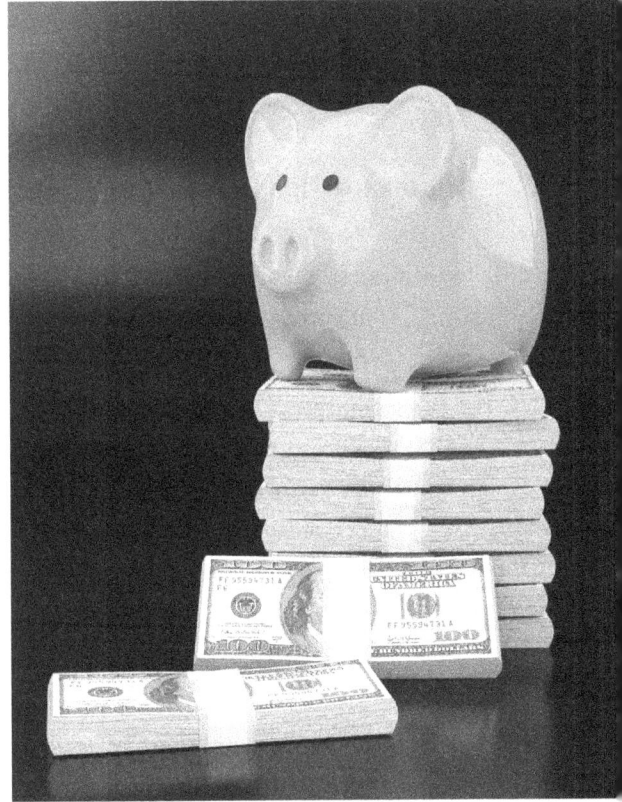

Fees, fees, and more fees

The people and the companies that run the investment plans need to get paid, just like you. There are several different ways they can be paid, but we will focus on the "standard" ones. Below are some of the fees normally associated with an employer retirement savings plan. Some of these may or may not be passed on to you, but most of the time they will.

- Administration fees: These may include recordkeeping, accounting, legal, and trustee services that are needed to run the plan.
- Investment fees: These are fees and expenses dealing with the actual management. Normally the fee is a percentage of the money you have invested. This can and will affect your returns.

- Individual service fees: In some cases, you may be charged for optional features that may be offered by the plan. For example, taking a loan out against your plan may generate an individual service fee.

Important Tips Before You Start Investing:

Address any outstanding consumer debt that you currently have. This will allow you to have more money to invest toward your future.

- If you have outstanding consumer debt but your company offers a company match, you may want to consider contributing at least up to the amount the company is matching, *only* if this is not going to cause any additional hardships for you. It is free money, after all.
- Do your research and understand what you're investing in before you invest your hard-earned money!
- Use dollar cost averaging to your advantage. Consistently investing a fixed amount on a fixed schedule regardless of the share price will allow you to buy more shares when the share price is lower, but fewer shares when the share prices are higher. This avoids dropping a large amount of cash at one time into an investment, thereby causing you to be a little or a lot uncomfortable. This also avoids the "timing the market" thought process.
- When investing, you want a "diversified portfolio," meaning you will be spreading your money across different types of industries, as well as across the different types of risk levels that you are comfortable with. This will minimize, or help "flatten," the highs and lows that come with investing in the stock market. Knowing that all your money is not tied up in one stock should give you peace of mind.
- You should only have around 10–15% of company stock in your portfolio. Minimizing the amount of company stock that you have is a way to protect yourself financially if anything were to happen to the company. This is a good thing, even if your company is a great company and has everything going for it. Why? You're most likely not on the board or part of the inner circle that makes the decisions on the direction of where the company is headed or whether the company is going to be bought out or go bankrupt. Look up Enron, and you will understand why having all your eggs in one basket is never a good idea. Look at a more recent example: General Electric (GE). It was one of the original members of the Dow Jones Industrial Average, but it has since been

removed after 111 years. At the time of being removed from the Dow, it had lost about 55% of its stock value. What if you worked for GE and had all of your retirement money wrapped up in GE stock? Over half of your retirement money would just be gone!

- If you are unsure of which investments you should pick, but you still want to invest, you may want to consider a targeted retirement fund option. This allows you to pick the year that you will most likely retire, and it's managed by the investment firm. The investments are adjusted from higher-risk to lower-risk investments as you get closer to the year you have chosen.

- A financial fiduciary is a must! A financial fiduciary is someone who is *only* acting in your best interest, both ethically and legally. Believe it or not, financial advisors are *not* required to put your interests above theirs. This is hard to believe, but it is true. Your best bet is a fee-only financial planner.

- A fee-only financial planner can review your current investments then make suggestions of possible changes you may need to make based on your financial goals. Their goal is to do a great job for you so you keep coming back for advice, not for investment products.

- Plan to live on only 4% of your retirement investments each year. Why? Well, by only living on 4% per year, you're leaving your "base investments" untouched, allowing it to grow while you are able to live off the interest from your investments for your day-to-day life, even for reinvesting.

- The Rule of 72 can help you estimate the number of years it will take to double your money. The formula is $72 \div R = Y$. "R" is the expected percentage rate of return. "Y" is the number of years it will take for your money to double.

- Suppose you invest $10,000 and you expected rate of return of 6%. Using the Rule of 72, it will take you 12 years to double your money. $72 \div 6\% = 12$ years.

Options as an employee

Your employer should offer you some type of employer-sponsored retirement plan you can participate in at some point. However, not all employer-sponsored retirement plans are created equal. Some are very low-cost plans while others will charge extremely high fees—meaning less money in your pocket when you're ready to retire.

Often employers will provide a "matching contribution" (free money) up to a certain percentage for those employees participating in the employer-sponsored retirement plan. If you have a low-cost employer-sponsored retirement plan, you want to use this to your financial advantage! Sometimes starting is the hardest part; making a jump from 0% to 15% can be overwhelming. Start out small by contributing 1%, then every 6 months contribute an additional 1%, and continue to do this until you're contributing 15% or 20% of your paycheck into your employer-sponsored retirement plan. *This is assuming that your employer-sponsored retirement plan is a low-cost plan!*

If your employer-sponsored retirement plan is charging 1% or above, you need to look at funding your own retirement outside of your employer-sponsored retirement plan. That being said, if your employer provides a "matching contribution" (free money) *contribute up to the match* before saving outside of the employer's plan. You're getting free money, so take advantage of it.

You're probably thinking, *Why? Most people think that 1% is not a lot of money for someone else to manage my money and take care of it for me, so what's the big deal?*

Well, right now you may not have a lot of money invested in your retirement plan, so 1% may not sound like much, but over time, it will make a serious difference in your wallet.

Below is an example of investment fees. Depending on the number of investments you have, the fees can add up quickly, leaving you with a lot less than you thought you would have. Other fees may also apply.

Take a look at how much money you're giving away with a standard run-of-the-mill retirement plan.

- 1% of $5,000 = $50 in fees, leaving you with $4,950.
- 1% of $50,000 = $500 in fees, leaving you with $49,500.
- 1% of $500,000 = $5,000 in fees, leaving you with $495,000.

As you can see, over time, your investments go up, but so do your fees. That 1% will lower the amount you have saved for retirement. In some cases, you will need to work an additional 7–10 years to make up for the 1% management fee that seemed like a good idea. Remember, whether your investments do well or not, the retirement plan always takes their 1%. Let's take a look at how much more money you will keep in your pocket when using a low-cost plan (other fees may apply).

- .20% of $5,000 = $10 in fees, leaving you with $4,990.
- .20% of $50,000 = $100 in fees, leaving you with $49,900.
- .20% of $500,000 = $1,000 in fees, leaving you with $499,000.

As you can see, a low-cost plan can leave you with almost all the money that you invested, allowing more of your money to make you money.

Types of employer-sponsored retirement plans

A lot of different types of employer-sponsored retirement plans are out there, and it can get a little confusing for most of us who don't deal with them on a regular basis.

WARNING! WARNING! WARNING! WARNING! WARNING! WARNING! WARNING! WARNING!

This is a warning for women!

One topic that is not often examined and talked about even less is women saving for retirement. Women so often give selflessly, taking care of others first and not even thinking twice about it. Stepping away from the workforce to raise children is one of the most selfless acts women can do for themselves and their family. But what about you? Who is or who will be taking care of you? Whether you're single or married, you as a woman need to save for *your own retirement*.

Do not rely on others to do the work for you. It is up to you! You need to know how investing works. If you are going to step away from the workforce, you will need to save *more* money, in a shorter amount of time, than a man will. During that time away from the workforce, you are most likely not investing, so you're falling behind. In addition to that, women typically live longer than men, so it is that much more important for you to save for retirement.

> One of the reasons I felt this needed to be highlighted is because of my mom. She told me the topic of how to handle money was just not talked about back when she was getting started in her working career. While this has gotten better over time, this still needs to get better, and women need get more involved with their own finances.

Disclaimer

I am not a licensed financial planner, retirement specialist, or stock broker, nor am I giving you any direction on how you should invest your money or anyone else's. You are responsible for your own research and making your own financial investment decisions.

Rules as well as the tax code change on a regular basis. Always consult your plan's administrator, accountant, and tax preparer for any changes that may apply to any of your retirement or investment accounts for your situation.

General notes

Always check with your plan's administrator for additional details with regard to your specific plan, as each plan is different. Always check with your plan's administrator before transferring, withdrawing, or making changes to ensure you are not going to be taxed, penalized, or charged a fee for your actions.

Retirement plans normally have both employer and/or employee contribution limits in addition to maximum income limits.

- Most plans have age 50 and over catch-up contributions.
- All have age 72 required minimum distribution.
- All retirement accounts have early withdrawals, taxes, and penalties (before age 59½).

- You always have the option to use the trustee-to-trustee transfer process to move your money from an old plan (meaning you no longer work for that employer) to a new plan (meaning a qualified plan of your choosing or to your new employer's plan) to avoid taxes and penalties associated with an early withdrawal.

- For those earning more than $250,000, it makes the most sense to choose the standard 401(k). You will most likely have lower income when you retire, meaning you will be taxed at a lower tax bracket than you are now.

- Around age 50, choosing between a traditional 401(k) and a Roth 401(k) is not as one-sided as it would be if you were in your 20s [Roth 401(k)], so either option could be a good choice depending on your situation.

401(k) Plan

A 401(k) plan is the most common employer-sponsored retirement plan offered today. A 401(k) plan is a *defined-contribution plan*, meaning you, your employer, or both make contributions on a regular basis. A 401(k) plan is a "tax-deferred" plan, meaning any contributions invested into the plan are done before any taxes have been paid on the contributions. Taxes will be paid on the money at the time it is withdrawn from your 401(k) in retirement.

Let's look at an example to make it a little easier. Say you decide to contribute $200 into your 401(k) out of each paycheck. Suppose your paycheck is $1,000. The first $200 will be taken off the top and sent to your 401(k) plan *before* any taxes have been applied to your paycheck. You will now only be paying taxes on the remaining $800 of your paycheck. That likely leaves you with $625 after taxes. When you retire and start to take distributions from your 401(k), you will then be taxed on the amounts that were withdrawn (distributed). This is the "tax-deferred" part of the 401(k) plan. At the time of retirement, you should be in a much lower tax bracket than when you were working. The money you withdraw will be taxed as ordinary income, typically at a much lower rate. This means you will be keeping more of the money you withdrew.

1. You could be 100% vested immediately in your 401(k), or it could stretch out over several years, which means you may have to wait for employer contributions to become yours.

2. If you were to lose or change jobs, you have 4 options with your existing 401(k).

   - **Option 1:** Keep your funds in your old employer's 401(k) plan, but you will not be able to contribute to it anymore.

   - **Option 2:** Transfer your funds into your new employer's 401(k) plan.

   - **Option 3:** Transfer your funds into an IRA (individual retirement account) that you have to set up with a low-cost investment provider.

   - **Option 4:** Receive a check, but 30% will be withheld—20% for taxes and 10% for penalties (if you are under age 59½).

Options 2 and 3 will need to be transferred by a process called a trustee-to-trustee transfer. This can be handled by your new plan's administrator to avoid the 30% tax and penalties that would be withheld if you chose to receive a check. If you choose to receive a check, things will get messy. Before doing any withdrawals or distributions, consult your plan's administrator and your accountant. Always ask first.

Roth 401(k) Plan

A newer and in most cases better plan (at least in my opinion), is the Roth 401(k). Some employers may not even be aware this option is available. Make sure to ask your employer or the plan's administrator of your current 401(k) if there's a Roth 401(k) option available. Roth 401(k) contributions are made after your income has been taxed. This means that at the time of retirement, when you withdraw any money, you will *not* be taxed. This is because the contributions were taxed before they went into your Roth 401(k). This allows all the earnings to be tax-free! How awesome is that?

Let's look at an example to make it a little easier. You decide to contribute $200 into your Roth 401(k) out of each paycheck. Your paycheck is $1,000. You will be taxed on your entire paycheck first, and that leaves you with $750 after taxes. Now your $200 Roth 401(k) contribution would be taken out, leaving you with $550 in take-home pay. As you can see, your take-home pay will be a little less than with the *standard* 401(k). However, when you retire and start to take distributions from your Roth 401(k), no taxes will need to be paid on any of those distributions!

> If your employer provides matching funds, the employer's contribution will be placed into a regular 401(k) and not into the Roth 401(k).
>
> You could be 100% vested immediately, or it could stretch out over several years, which means you may have to wait for employer contributions to become yours.
>
> Early "contribution" withdrawals from your Roth 401(k) will *not be taxed or penalized.* The gains must be left in the account, or taxes and penalties will be applied.

Say you have put in $50,000 into your Roth. To clarify this a little more, say you have contributed (paid in) $50,000 into your Roth IRA. All that money you contributed was taxed *before* it went into your Roth IRA. Only the money that you have contributed could be withdrawn tax- and penalty-free. Say the Roth IRA balance was $60,000. If you were to withdraw any amount over your contributions ($50,000), taxes and penalties would be applied, as this money is considered earnings. *However, your plan may apply early withdrawal fees of their own.*

Dirk says . . .

**IT'S NOT HOW MUCH YOU EARN;
IT'S HOW MUCH YOU SAVE.
HOW MANY TIMES HAVE YOU HEARD
A NEWS STORY OF A PROFESSIONAL ATHLETE
WHO MADE MILLIONS AND IS NOW BROKE?
IT'S NOT ABOUT HOW MUCH YOU MAKE!**

403(b) Plan

A 403(b) plan is almost the same as a 401(k) plan, but it is designed for nonprofit organizations. These include hospitals, home health service agencies, public school systems, churches, associations of churches, and welfare service agencies. The 403(b) plan tends to have multiple layers of fees that you need to be aware of up front, especially if it is managed by an insurance company. You could have as much as 25% in fees compared to some in a typical 401(k) plan, meaning less for you in retirement. You may be better off just setting up a Roth IRA instead.

> Normally the employee is the sole contributor to this type of plan, and contributions are tax deductible when made. Your employer can match your contributions up to a certain percentage.
>
> The earnings from your investments are tax-deferred, and the same contribution limits apply as those of 401(k) plans.

457 Plan

A 457 plan works the same way as a 401(k) plan but is designed for state and local government employees. Both plans have the same contribution limits. However, there is one major difference between a 457 plan and a 401(k) plan.

> If the employer offers both a 457 plan and a 401(k) plan, the employee can fully contribute to both plans! This allows the employee to make double the contributions! Wow, that is awesome!

Thrift Savings Plan (TSP)

A thrift savings plan (TSP) is a retirement savings plan for Federal employees and military personnel including the Ready Reserve. This is a *defined-contribution plan*. You are able to choose one of two types of TSPs. The first is a tax-deferred or traditional TSP, similar to an employer-sponsored 401(k) plan. The second is a Roth TSP, similarly to an employer-sponsored Roth 401(k) plan.

There are only six different types of funds that you can invest within the TSP:
- Government Securities Investment – (G) Fund
- Fixed Income Index Investment – (F) Fund
- Common Stock Index Investment – (C) Fund
- Small Capitalization Stock Index Investment – (S) Fund

- International Stock Index Investment – (I) Fund
- Life Cycle – (L) Fund

Blended Retirement System (BRS)

A new retirement savings plan for the military is the Blended Retirement System or BRS. The BRS has components of both the traditional legacy retirement pension plan a "defined benefit" with a defined contribution into your TSP. As a new active service member, you will be automatically enrolled in the BRS after January 1, 2018, with 3% of your base pay invested into an age-appropriate life cycle – (L) Fund within your TSP after 60 days of service. The government will automatically contribute 1% up to an additional 4% if you increase your contributions.

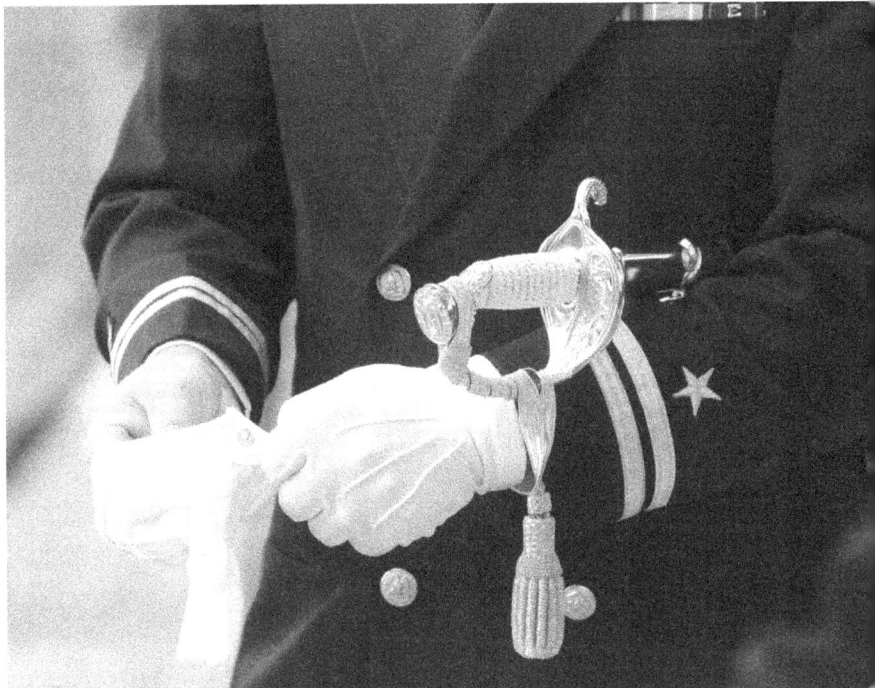

SIMPLE IRA Plan

Savings Incentive Match Plan for Employees or SIMPLE, is an IRA (individual retirement account) plan offered by an employer. Smaller employers typically choose this type of plan as it is less costly for them.

When participating in a SIMPLE IRA plan, your contributions are tax deductible, meaning the amount that you contribute is subtracted from your gross income (pretax income), which lowers your taxable income by the amount you contributed to your SIMPLE IRA. With the SIMPLE IRA, an employer must make either matching contributions up to 3% of the employee's salary or non-elective contributions. Nonelective contributions are funds employers can choose to contribute toward an eligible employee's employer-sponsored retirement plan regardless of whether employees make their own contributions.

Below is an example of how contributions and taxes are applied to your income with a SIMPLE plan.

- Your gross income is $5,000 (income before being taxed: pretax income).
- The amount you are contributing to your SIMPLE plan is $1,000 (taxed when withdrawn in retirement: tax-deferred).
- Your new gross income amount that will be taxed that year is $4,000 (lowered taxable income).

> You could be 100% vested immediately, or it could stretch out over several years, which means you may have to wait for employer contributions to become yours.

SEP IRA Plan

Simplified employee pension (or SEP) is another IRA (individual retirement account)-based retirement plan that can be offered by your employer. This allows *only* your employer to contribute to your retirement IRA. Smaller employers often choose this type of plan as it is a very simple way of administering a retirement plan for their employees and is less costly than other retirement plans. That being said, a business of any size can establish a SEP. Even those of you who are self-employed can set up your own SEP.

A SEP is an IRA, and the distribution and rollover requirements are the same as traditional IRA; however, the contribution limits are much higher than those with a run-of-the-mill IRA.

Contributions are still limited, but it is an either/or choice of the lesser amount:

- $57,000 for 2020 (the maximum any employee can contribute to all retirement plans combined)
- 25% of compensation

> SEP IRA plans *do not* allow you to make catch-up contributions.

> You are 100% vested as soon as the money is deposited into your account, which means you do not have to wait several years before the employer contributions are yours.

Defined Benefit Pension Plans

This type of plan is nice if you can get it, but it is rare, and at some point will go extinct. It is also referred to as the traditional retirement plan. A defined benefit pension plan is exactly that: defined benefits. You will receive a fixed monthly benefit (money) once you retire, without having to make any contributions to the plan. The employer is typically the sole contributor to this type of plan.

> The benefit is based on your income and years of service.
>
> All investment decisions will be made by the employer, not the employee. The plan is entirely administered by your employer, so you will have no control over the funds upon reaching retirement age.
>
> The plan will set a "normal retirement age," which is when you will be eligible to receive (or begin to receive, in the case of annuity or installment payments) your full accrued benefit.

Other types of employer-offered retirement options

Below are options that may not be offered by your current employer but are still good to be aware of as they may be available from your next employer.

Employee stock ownership plans (ESOPs), money purchase plan, profit-sharing plan or a payroll deduction IRA.

Real Estate

Real estate investing has and always will be popular as a go-to investment. There are a lot of people that do very well, but there are also a lot of people that lose everything. Real Estate is risky, especially if you don't know what you're doing, haven't done your research, and you don't have any cash on hand. Borrowing to invest is extremely risky; you will have the obligation to pay your loan back even if you're not generating any income from that investment.

Always avoid those Free Real Estate Seminars that are going to share the secret or system that can make you a real estate mogul. Their goal is to sell you their system, and it almost always involves you borrowing money.

There are multiple ways to invest in real estate, but probably the easiest way to dip your toe into the world of real estate investing is with Real Estate Investment Trust, or more commonly known as a REIT. They are funds that typically specialize in a specific real estate sector. Individuals are allowed to buy shares in commercial real estate portfolios that receive income from a variety of properties, including office buildings, hotels, data centers, healthcare facilities, apartment complexes, and many other types of properties.

With a REIT, you're able to start investing with a much smaller amount of money, but it's money you have on hand. This avoids you going into debt in order to invest in real estate.

Again you must do your research before investing.

Non-Employer-Sponsored Retirement Options

IRA

An individual retirement account (IRA) is an investment account that allows you to invest money for retirement and can have possible tax advantages. With an IRA, you are able to invest in stocks, bonds, and mutual funds. You can set up different types of IRAs. The first is a traditional IRA, and the second is a Roth IRA.

Traditional IRA

With a traditional IRA (not employer sponsored), your contributions are in most cases tax deductible up to the IRS limits. This means your original contributions will be made after you have been taxed on your gross income, but the deduction will be made when you file your taxes. The amount you contributed to your traditional IRA in that year would be deducted from your gross income, so you would be taxed on the lower amount.

> **Example**
>
> Suppose your gross income for the year is $45,000 (before taxes) and you contributed $5,000 to your traditional IRA (not employer sponsored). Your new gross taxable income would be $40,000 when filing your taxes for that year. The $5,000 contribution is shown as a deduction in the paperwork when filing your taxes. This is known as an adjusted gross income (AGI).

Roth IRA

Contributions to your Roth IRA are not tax deductible! Unlike the traditional IRA, you are not able to adjust your gross income when filing your yearly taxes. This may not seem like a good thing, but it's actually really awesome. Here's why—all the money that was invested and all of the growth (earnings) are not taxed when you withdraw money in retirement! How awesome is that?

Let's run the numbers so we can see what that means.

Say you have invested $250,000 over 50 years into your Roth IRA. Over that time, your investment has grown to $1,250,000. That in itself is awesome, but the $1,000,000 of growth (earnings) is not taxable! Think about that for a while. Pretty awesome, right?

> If you have an income below $50,000, a Roth IRA is a good choice over the traditional IRA.
>
> Early "contribution" withdrawals from your Roth 401(k) will *not be taxed or penalized*. The gains must be left in the account or taxes and penalties will be applied. This is normally around 30% of the amount that is withdrawn of the growth (earnings). To clarify this a little more, say you have contributed (paid in) $50,000 into your Roth IRA. All that money you contributed was taxed *before* it went into your Roth IRA. Only the money that you have contributed could be withdrawn tax and penalty free. Say the Roth IRA balance was $60,000. If you were to withdraw any amount over your contributions ($50,000) taxes and penalties would be applied, as this money is considered earnings.

Spousal IRA Contribution

For couples that are legally married and are filing jointly, a set of IRS rules allows a non-working spouse to contribute to their own IRA or Roth IRA as long as it falls within the IRS income limits. Please consult your tax advisor and/or your accountant for more details.

Nondeductible IRA

Nondeductible IRA contributions are just that: nondeductible! When you file your taxes, your contributions will not be deducted from your gross income. This can be used for several reasons. You are a high-income earner, and it exceeds specific IRS limits, and you have a retirement plan at work.

- You don't have a retirement plan at work, but your spouse does.
- You want to move money into a Roth IRA (a back-door Roth).
- You want easy access to cash and you are 59½ or older but still want your investments to grow tax-deferred.

Max out all of your IRA contribution options first.

Non-Retirement Investing

Chances are that you will need to open a brokerage account with a brokerage or broker in order to start investing in non-retirement investments. What is a brokerage? In this case it is a company that buys and sells stocks, bonds, mutual funds, securities, commodities, and exchange-traded funds (ETFs). What is a brokerage account? It is an account that gives you the ability to buy and sell stocks, bonds, mutual funds, securities, commodities, and ETFs on the stock exchange. There are a few ways to invest without a brokerage account, but to make it a little easier on yourself, just stick with a brokerage account.

And of course, there is not just one type of broker or just one type of brokerage account. Oh, no—that would make it way too easy for us mere mortals.

Types of Brokerages

Full-Service Brokerages
Normally, they do the research, advise you on which changes should be made to your portfolio, and manage your transactions and investments for you. This comes at a full-service price (high commissions).

Discount Brokerages
These offer much lower prices (low commissions) than full-service brokerages. Most of them offer access to financial advisors and also provide research.

Free or Almost Free Brokerages
Yes, that's right, they do exist. But they have limitations, restrictions, and can require a large minimum investment, sometimes as much as $10,000. You also may not have access to mutual funds or bonds.

Dirk says . . .

YOU CANNOT AND SHOULD NOT EXPECT OTHERS TO GIVE YOU MONEY FOR YOUR RETIREMENT. YOU ARE THE ONE IN CONTROL AND NO ONE ELSE. YOU CANNOT COUNT ON YOUR PARENTS, GRANDPARENTS, CHILDREN, FRIENDS, THE GOVERNMENT, THE LOTTERY, OR AN INHERITANCE TO GET YOU OUT OF DEBT OR FUND YOUR RETIREMENT.

Types of Brokerage Accounts

Taxable Accounts

This is the most common type of account offered by most brokerage firms. You're able to buy and sell securities, meaning stocks, bonds, options, contracts, and shares of mutual funds.

Tax-Advantaged Accounts

These are accounts such as IRAs, both traditional and Roth, as well as 401(k)s.

Cash versus Margin Accounts

Usually, when you open a new brokerage account, you will need to choose whether the account will be a cash account or a margin account. A cash account will require you to deposit money into your brokerage account in order for you to buy securities. This is the simplest and easiest to understand. If you have money in your account, you can buy securities. If not, you cannot.

A margin account is an account where you can borrow money from the brokerage to buy securities "on margin." You may have heard of a "margin call." This means the brokerage firm is demanding that you deposit cash into your account to cover possible losses. This can be very risky, and you must have the cash on hand to cover a "margin call" that could happen at any time.

> You may be pitched something called "private placements." These are very profitable for the broker but not very good for your wallet. They are easy to get into but almost impossible to get out of, so stay away from them.

Non-Retirement Savings Options

This is just your run-of-the-mill savings, money market account, or CD (certificate of deposit) for short-term savings goals. This is normally for 0–5 years. They are easily accessible, with no risk and with very little or no reward, but your money is safe as long as you are below the FDIC or NCUA insured amounts at a single institution.

Online Savings

Often you will get a much better interest-bearing rate from online-only banks or credit unions than you will at a traditional physical bank or credit union. Either one is fine to just park your cash for a short time.

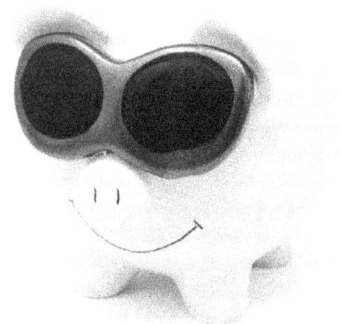

Certificate of Deposit (CD)

A certificate of deposit (CD) (and no, it's not that shiny disk that went into the thin slot in your car radio back in the day) offers higher interest than a savings account but comes with some drawbacks. You will need to deposit a minimum amount of money for a fixed amount of time, in return for a specific interest rate. Another drawback is that an early withdrawal penalty will be enforced.

Social Security

As you can see, I have left Social Security as the last option to cover! This is for a reason, of course. The hope was to show you the possibilities available to you and show you that it's not as complicated as you may think. The other hope was that you will start planning for your retirement and not choose to depend on the promise of the government to take care of you when you need it most. Taking the first step to controlling your retirement is up to you—you just need to take action. That being said, let's take a look at that Social Security retirement benefit.

- In order to start receiving a Social Security retirement benefit, you must be 62 years of age, but the benefit you will receive is 30% less than if you waited until your full retirement at age 67. Other than a cost-of-living adjustment (COLA), your base benefit will not increase! Currently, the Social Security retirement benefit at age 62 is around $953 a month, only $11,436 a year. Imagine: $953 a month! Can you live on that? If I had to guess, I would say probably not! In general, I bet you're surprised at how little your Social Security retirement benefit will pay you each month.
- Full retirement age is currently 66 years of age, at which time you will receive your full Social Security retirement benefit around $1,300 per month. That is only $15,600 a year. That's not much better, and I bet you couldn't live on that amount alone and cover all your bills. The full retirement age will continue to rise over time and could change for those that are close but not yet retired.
- If you're able to delay taking your Social Security retirement benefit until age 70, you will receive around $1,681 per month. That's only $20,172 a year. That's a little better, but I bet you still couldn't live on that amount alone and cover all your bills. If you're thinking that the longer you wait, the more you will get, this is true to a point. However, your benefits will no longer increase after age 70.

As you can see, your Social Security retirement benefit goes up by 8% for each year you delay taking it.

The Social Security Trust Fund is paying out more than it is taking in, which is not good for those of you who are counting on Social Security. The current estimate is that full benefits will be able to be paid out until 2034, at which time the fund will run out of treasury bonds to redeem. Then it will have to reduce the benefits that it can provide or raise the retirement age—or both.

> The Social Security Administration has several other benefit programs that may be available to you beyond your retirement benefits. Take some time and look into them as they may help you out financially. Do a quick web search for Social Security Administration (www.ssa.gov) or even go down to your local Social Security Administration office and talk to someone in person for more attention.

WARNING! WARNING! WARNING! WARNING! WARNING! WARNING! WARNING! WARNING!

CAUTION! CAUTION! CAUTION! CAUTION! CAUTION! CAUTION! CAUTION! CAUTION!

Annuity

In almost all cases, you should run away, far away, from anyone trying to sell you an annuity! Hopefully, you got the hint from the *warning* and *caution* banners above. Annuities are a little more complex than other "investments." I put investments in quotes as annuities are normally pitched as an "investment," but they are actually an *insurance contract*. As with any other insurance, you are transferring risk from yourself to the insurer. That's exactly what you're doing with an annuity. These are marketed as safe and guaranteed income for those looking for a consistent stream of income.

As with other legal documents, once it is signed, it obligates you and the insurance company to each other until the contract is fulfilled. Breaking the contract will result in extremely high surrender charges (fees) that can span a time frame of 5–15 years before no surrender charges would apply to you.

Nearly always, annuities are only good for the person who is *selling* the annuity. Annuities have extremely high sales commissions attached to them, and that is never a good thing for your wallet.

I would pose this question to show you how weird an annuity setup is:

Would you go to an auto mechanic to get your tooth fixed?

You wouldn't, would you? You wouldn't ask your investment brokerage to sell you insurance for your home, would you? No? Then why would you invest through an insurance company? They both have their specialties, and that's what they are best at, so keep them separate. Keep it simple. Keep them separate. Invest using low-cost investment firms, and buy insurance from an insurance company. This will work out the best for you in the long run.

Types of Annuities

These are some of the types of annuities:

- Fixed annuity
- Variable annuity
- Fixed indexed annuity
- Immediate annuity
- Deferred annuity

The only annuity that would likely have a benefit to you would be an immediate annuity.

Immediate Annuity

This is still an insurance product, not an investment! Usually, immediate annuities have very low commissions, meaning the salesperson is not likely to push this product or will even try to steer you away from it, as it does not fatten their wallet.

For an immediate annuity, you will need to provide a lump sum of cash up front in order for it to guarantee a stream of income for the rest of your life. Obviously, the amount you pay up front and the options you choose will determine the amount you will be paid each month, over a period of time, or if specific conditions are met.

Immediate Annuity Options

Below are the most common options but not necessarily all of them.

Life

Pays you a fixed monthly amount until you die.

Life with cash refund

Pays you a fixed monthly amount until you die, then pays your beneficiaries the remaining amount of your lump sum if you have not used it completely.

Period Certain

Only pays you for a specified amount of time, such as 10, 15, or 20 years. Life and Period Certain pay you a fixed monthly amount until you die, but if you die within a specified period, then your beneficiaries will receive monthly payments until the period certain portion has run out.

Joint Annuities

This applies to two people, not just one.

Variable Immediate Annuity

Part of your lump sum is put into a *true* investment such as a mutual fund that could increase your monthly payments if the investment increases in value.

Inflation-Protected Annuities

Inflation-Protected Annuities are a hedge against inflation and are used to maintain the buying power of the annuity. Some may refer to it as a cost-of-living adjustment (COLA). These are sometimes offered as a rider (optional coverage with additional terms and conditions) to the annuity.

NUTSHELL

Retirement planning and investing can be complex and confusing for young and old alike. Keep it simple. Reduce and eliminate your debt, live on less than you make, and invest. This is the foundation for an early and comfortable retirement. "Trust but verify" is a good motto to live by when someone is trying to "sell you an investment." Understand which retirement options are available to you through your employer and outside of your employer.

If you do not understand it, do not invest in it until you do. Ask for help from a financial fiduciary fee-only financial planner. Wow, that is a mouthful! They have your best interests in mind because they want you to keep coming back for years and years to come, and that can only happen if they do a great job for you. Take your time to find the one who meets your needs.

Take advantage of your employer's contribution match (free money). Invest using a low-cost investment brokerage firm, not a full-commissioned brokerage firm. Keeping the fees below 1% is key to keeping more of your money over time. You will be able to retire earlier as a result.

Women, whether you are single or married, you need to save for *your own retirement*. Do not rely on others to do the work for you. It is up to you! You need to know how investing works. If you are going to step away from the workforce, you will need to save *more* money, in a shorter amount of time than a man. During that time away from the workforce, you are most likely not investing, so you're falling behind. In addition to that, women typically live longer than men, so it is that much more important for you to save for retirement!

For more information, see irs.gov/retirement-plans/plan-sponsor/types-of-retirement-plans

CHAPTER 22

The Crossover

(Funerals and Burials)

WELL, ALL GOOD THINGS must come to an end. At some point, we are all going to die. This can be a difficult subject to bring up, let alone talk about or plan for in advance, but at some point, in the future, you will need to discuss your death and make decisions for that time in addition to writing your last will and testament. If you plan ahead, you can save yourself and your loved ones a lot of financial decisions at a very emotional time.

> I was shocked at how much a funeral can cost. Unfortunately, my mother-in-law passed somewhat unexpectedly several years ago and dealing with the shock of her passing was one thing, but dealing with all of the decisions that had to be made within a short amount of time just compounded the grief. It was also a rude awakening on how things could go from bad to worse when you make financial decisions at a time when you're not thinking clearly.

Funerals and burials are expensive. The cost can range from $7,000–$10,000 but can go way beyond that if the decisions are made during this emotional time. This is not something you normally go shopping for on a regular basis to compare prices. This can cause you to overspend. This cost can be an additional burden to your loved ones that they didn't expect if the details have not been planned for in advance.

> A surprising fact is that in most states, you are not legally required to use a funeral home to conduct a funeral. There are legal requirements involved, though, and usually it's just easier to have the professionals handle this when it happens unexpectedly.

The cost for funerals and burials can add up quickly, so plan ahead to help everyone involved. That way, you get what you want with no additional stress on your family during the time of sadness. This will also allow them to focus on being there for one another, not on making decisions about your funeral arrangements. Comparison shop, because it's still your money, and you may want to pass some of it on to your family or your favorite charity. Planning ahead allows you to pass more of it on when you pass on.

The Federal Trade Commission (FTC) has created The Funeral Rule that allows you to choose only those goods and services you want and to pay only for those you have selected.

There are several options to reduce or eliminate the cost of funerals and burials.

Home Funeral

This practice was very common before the 20th century and is still legal in most states. You will need to fill out the proper paperwork with the help of the medical examiner or doctor to make sure everything is completed properly.

Home Burial

This may not be for everyone, but it's still an option. You will need to meet the legal requirements set by your state. California, Indiana, and Washington prohibit home burials, and all other states have regulations around home burial.

Nonprofit Memorial Society

These have a very small (one-time) membership fee of $25–$35 (depending on your state). They are able to use group buying power to reduce your cost by about 75%. This brings your funeral and burial costs down to around $1,750–$2,500.

> Avoid prepaying for funeral and burial services. Many things can happen between the time you make your arrangements and when you die. You could move, the operator could sell the business and never put the money into escrow, or the operator could go out of business.

Embalming

Embalming is not required by all states, but that does not mean the funeral home is going to tell you that. By skipping the embalming process, you can save hundreds of dollars.

Casket

Provide your own casket. Funeral homes must accept a casket that you provide. This can save thousands of dollars.

> Skip the special casket or something marketed as a "protective casket." You could pay upwards of $800 or more for a $7 item.

Cremation

A direct cremation cost can start at as little as $550, and on the high end can be around $1,500. A direct cremation is when you are transferred from the place of passing directly to the crematory. No viewing will take place, and a funeral home or burial is not required.

For Science

Donating your body to science is one way to eliminate all costs of a funeral and burial, as long as it's arranged ahead of time. You will get door-to-door service as long as someone makes the call for you. Universities and medical schools are always in need of donations, so take advantage of this.

NUTSHELL

While our own death is not something we want to think about, it's going to happen. Planning ahead will make it less stressful for your family during a time of sadness. It will also allow them to focus on being there for one another, not on making decisions about your funeral arrangements. With funeral costs ranging from $7,000–$10,000 or more, it's not a burden you want them to worry about paying. By choosing to join a nonprofit memorial society, price comparing funeral home services, skipping embalming, providing your own casket, cremation, or donating your body to science, you can reduce that cost by 75% or even get it for free.

CHAPTER 23

Now What?
Your Definition of
Financial Success
Revisited

YOU ARE ALMOST FINISHED with *The Quick-Start Guide to Financial Success*. Has your definition or vision of financial success changed after reading this book? Do you need to change a few things? If not, that is great. If so, that is okay, too.

The area below is for you to revise your definition or vision of what financial success looks like to *you* now.

Current Date: _____

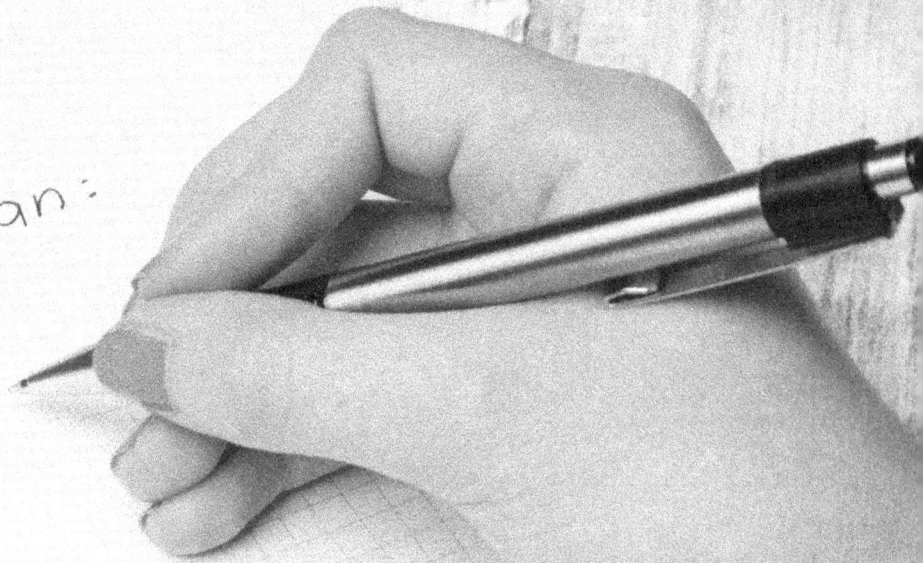

My Plan:

CHAPTER 24

What's Your Plan?

WHAT'S YOUR PLAN TO reach *your* definition or vision of financial success? Now that you have read *The Quick-Start Guide to Financial Success* and you have the basics down for changing your mindset, creating a budget, and making good financial decisions, you need a plan. What's yours?

The next two pages are for you to state your plan to get out of debt and reach your definition or vision of financial success. Make sure you review your plan on a regular basis to keep your plan in the forefront of your mind. Later you can always revisit your plan, and make changes as needed because it will change over time.

Current Date: _____

The Next Challenge

Congratulations! You have read the entire book from cover to cover. The real test is being able to use the knowledge you have gained to make changes that will make you financially successful.

When will you take your first step toward financial success?

WHY NOT START NOW?

YOU ARE WORTH IT!

For more information and resources from the book, visit:

DirkWrites.com

P.S. – Don't forget to sign up for the Inside Scoop and receive a FREE copy of my budget and FREE copy of the How to Choose a House Checklist!

P.P.S. – Thank you for taking the time to read my book and I hope it has helped you in small way. I would be grateful if you would leave a review or comment so other people could benefit of your experience, insight, and impact on your life from reading this book.

Thanks again.

—Dirk

Align your company's vision of success by equipping everyone on your team with a prosperity mindset.

Contact Dirk for your next company event via:

DirkTalks.com

www.ingramcontent.com/pod-product-compliance
Lightning Source LLC
Chambersburg PA
CBHW051754200326
41597CB00025B/4546